Gutter Humor

Gutter Humor

Outrageous But True Bowling Stories

From the Files of the National Bowling Hall of Fame and Museum

Bruce Nash and Allan Zullo

Andrews and McMeel • *A Universal Press Syndicate Company* • Kansas City

Designed by Rick Cusick
Illustrations by Paul Coker

Library of Congress Cataloging-in-Publication Data

Nash, Bruce M.
      Gutter humor : outrageous but true bowling stories / Bruce Nash
   and Allan Zullo.
         p. cm.
      "From the files of the National Bowling Hall of Fame and Museum."
      ISBN 0-8362-1745-4
      1. Bowling--Humor. 2. Bowling--Anecdotes. I. Zullo, Allan.
   II. Title.
   GV904.N37   1994   94-1676
   794.6'0207--dc20

ATTENTION: SCHOOLS AND BUSINESSES
Andrews and McMeel books are available at quantity discounts with bulk purchase
for educational, business, or sales promotional use. For information, please write to:
Special Sales Department, Andrews and McMeel
4900 Main Street
Kansas City, Missouri 64112

Dedication

To my "roll" model, Mark Zakarin, a straight shooter who proved you could strike from the Brooklyn side and bowl 'em over in Hollywood.
　　　　　　　　　　　—Bruce Nash

To Ray Tufts, who's had more than his share of 7–10 splits in life but still knows how to pick up those spares.
　　　　　　　　　　　—Allan Zullo

Acknowledgments

We couldn't have put this book together without the capable assistance of several outstanding individuals and their organizations.

John Dalzell, of the National Bowling Hall of Fame and Museum in St. Louis, helped provide the bulk of the initial research. We are especially grateful to him and to Hall of Fame executive director Gerald Baltz for their cooperation.

Many thanks go to Mark Miller of the American Bowling Congress (ABC), Bobby Dinkins of the Professional Bowlers Association (PBA), and to Karl Lueders and Jim Dressel of *Bowlers Journal International* for providing us with vital information.

Among bowling writers who lent invaluable assistance were: Tom Fowler, Dawson Taylor, Chuck Otterson, and the late Lou Marks. We also thank Frank Centolella for his help.

Contents

Reading the Lanes

Ever since 1895 when the American Bowling Congress standardized the rules and equipment, bowling has remained virtually unchanged. Bowlers still jump for joy with every strike and moan with every split. They still gloat when winning the kitty and grumble when paying for the beer frame. They still rejoice over love taps and curse over 10-pin taps.

When it comes to incredible incidents, hilarious happenings, fantastic feats, and remarkable records, bowling is in a league by itself. Like the bowler who racked up ten strikes—and failed to break 200. Or the poor soul who achieved ignoble immortality by rolling the lowest score ever in ABC competition—a pitiful 2. Or the kegler who knocked down the entire back row of pins on his first ball—but left the other six pins standing.

Bowling has had its bizarre moments outside the alley, too. There was the bowler who was knocked out by his own ball . . . the unlucky guy whose wayward ball caused an auto accident . . . and the fugitive who was arrested because she bowled too well.

And let's not forget the zany characters of the game, from the notorious hustler Count Gengler, who conned marks by wearing a top hat and tails to the bowling alley and pretending he couldn't bowl . . . to Hall of Famer Paul Krumske, who sometimes faked a heart attack to unnerve his opponent . . . to Ernie Schlegel who, during his hustling days, would pour a shot of bourbon over his head and act drunk to sucker bowlers into high stakes games that he always won.

Gutter Humor is a fun-filled celebration of bowling's most amusing and amazing stories. We hope it will bowl you over with laughs — and surprises.

Pin-Demonium!

Crazy Tosses

Doing the Splits

Bowling has come up with some imaginative names for splits, such as Dime Store (5–10), Faith, Hope & Charity (2–7–10), Big Ears (4–7–10), Snake Eyes (7–10), and Three Stooges (5–7–10).

But there was no ready term for the split that John Dwarzski threw.

While competing in 1972 at the Bowl-O-Drome in Melvindale, Michigan, Dwarzski knocked down the entire back row of pins—but nothing else—on his first toss at a full rack!

His ball toppled the 7–8–9–10 but left standing intact the other six pins in front—the 1–2–3–4–5–6. The ball barely touched the 10-pin just before falling into the gutter, triggering a domino effect in the back row.

No one knew what to call the split other than "unbelievable!" Dwarzski's shot was so unique that the ABC and the Bowling Hall of Fame have no record of any bowler ever throwing one before or since.

* * *

The odds of converting a 7–10 split are estimated at one in 2,000,000. But on rare occasions, a bowler has actually knocked down the 7 and 10 on the first ball—leaving the other eight pins standing!

The odds of such a split are about one in 50,000,000.

Ed Schnettler, of St. Cloud, Minnesota, was the first bowler reported to have rolled a reverse Snake Eyes. In 1945, he was asked to fill in as a substitute on a Knights of Columbus team. Schnettler hadn't bowled in quite a while, so he was feeling a bit nervous and rusty on his first few tosses. Halfway through the game, he still hadn't collected any markers and no one was paying him much attention—until the sixth frame.

On his first toss in the sixth, Schnettler was determined to get a strike or at least a spare. He flung his ball harder than ever and then watched in dismay as it strayed left and headed for the corner. The ball missed all the pins but one, smashing into the 7-pin.

Incredibly, the pin flew into the pit, bounced off the kickback, and neatly took out the 10-pin on the other side without touching any of the other pins.

Although Schnettler knocked over the two hardest pins, he failed to get the spare on his next ball.

An ad in the December 20, 1914, Des Moines Register:
"WANTED: A bowler who can shoot tenpins following another bowler with a freak delivery. Anyone will do who will not watch the course of the ball of the person shooting just ahead of him. Apply to Captain Morrison of the Mission team."

The Eight Ball

Bowler Bill Ballinger scored a 14 in one frame—without making a marker!

In 1960, Ballinger was set to bowl his first ball in the tenth frame of the final game of a Tuesday night mixed league. He cranked up and let his ball rip down the lane. The ball smashed squarely into the head pin, leaving the dreaded Big Ears split of the 4–6–7–10.

But Ballinger didn't mind—not after what happened a few seconds later. One of the struck pins flew off the pin deck and gutter with such force that it bounced into the adjoining lane and knocked down another eight pins!

"I'll take a 14 on that ball," he deadpanned.

Ballinger finished the game with an official score of 202—or 210 if you count the extra pins.

Dead On Arrival

During a 1980 league game, Don Renfro tossed his ball down the alley like he had done hundreds of times before. He'd had his share of strikes and gutter balls and lucky shots. But nothing in his wildest dreams could prepare him for what was about to happen to his ball on this memorable night.

It hit the head pin and four others—and then stopped dead in the middle of the pins!

Renfro, president of the Berea Road Industrial League, was bowling at Hornack's Lanes in Berea, Ohio, when he tossed the strangest shot of his life. Renfro, a husky young man with a powerful throw, flung his sixteen-pound ball hard like he always did. Then he watched in amazement as the ball hit the pocket and, as if by magic, stopped among the pins and failed to fall into the pit.

The ball had cut a path through the middle of the tenpins, leaving an almost impossible Greek Church split of the 4–6–7–8–10. But, amazingly, the ball remained sitting where the 5-pin originally had been spotted.

Renfro's ball had achieved one of the rarest feats in all of bowling. When his ball hit the pins, it simply stopped after the 5-pin was momentarily caught between the ball and the pinsetting machine.

Recalled Bill Hornack, owner of the bowling center, "Don came up to me and said, 'Bill, my ball is stuck in the middle of the pins.' And I said, 'How could that happen?' I went over to his lane and sure enough there was the ball. I've never seen or heard of anything like it before or since in all my years in the bowling business. We were all scratching our heads, wondering how it had happened."

According to the National Bowling Hall of Fame, the odds of such an occurrence are more than 1 in 100,000,000.

* * *

Amazingly, that's not the first time a ball had stopped in the middle of the pins. But unlike Renfro's incredible toss, this ball was halted by a mechanical breakdown.

In 1971, Cary Schultz, of Orland Park, Illinois, fired his ball smack into the head pin. But the pin didn't topple over or roll off to one side of the pin deck. Instead it flew up and over the 2-pin and 3-pin and became lodged in the automatic pinsetter above, with the bottom part of the pin protruding from the machine.

It all happened so quickly—in a split second—that when the ball reached the middle of the rest of the pins, it came to a sudden halt, becoming jammed between the stuck head pin and the pin deck.

Since the oddity was ruled a dead ball, Schultz was allowed to bowl the frame over again—but only after the house mechanic spent an hour trying to free the ball and the lodged head pin.

Boomerang Ball

While trying for a strike, Dick Kittleson put a little bit too much spin on his ball—so much, in fact, that it rolled right back to him!

It happened in 1976 when Kittleson's Brooklyn Hit left the 4–7–8 split. The ball, however, did not fall into the pit. After mixing it up with the pins, the spinning ball skidded to a stop and then, incredibly, began slowly rolling back toward the stunned bowler.

To his astonishment, the ball rolled and rolled three-quarters of the way back up the lane before it fell into the gutter and finished its bizarre return trip to the foul line. After recovering from the shock, Kittleson picked up his ball—and then proceeded to convert the spare, finishing with a score of 189.

Lickety Split

Jack Miller defied the old bowler's superstition of never turning your back on a thrown ball until after it has hit the pins. As a consequence, Miller tossed one of the weirdest splits ever.

In 1960, Miller, of Green Bay, Wisconsin, was primed for fun when he stepped up to the lane for his first throw in the opening game of a league match. As soon as he released his ball, he watched for a second and saw that it was headed for what he thought was a perfect pocket shot.

So he confidently turned his back, which superstition says you should never do. Suddenly, Miller heard a strange sound as the ball hit the pins. He turned around and couldn't believe his eyes.

His ball had taken out only the center line of pins—the 1, 2, 5, and 9. He was left with the strangest split he had ever seen before—the 3–4–6–7–8–10! Needless to say, Miller failed to pick up the spare.

High Roller

Imagine throwing a ball that never touched the pins—and never went into the gutter. It's happened before.

During the 1964 National All-Star Duckpin Tournament at the Queenstown Bowl near Washington, D.C., Helen Hatch, of Richmond, Virginia, was gunning for a spare when the law of physics seemed to unravel. The ball rolled solidly toward the pocket when, to everyone's stunned amazement, it suddenly took flight! The ball flew over the pins, missing every one of them, and landed in the pit.

"Don't I get anything?" she asked in bewilderment.

It turned out that a piece of the pinsetter had fallen onto the lane during Helen's release and acted as a ramp, launching her ball into the air. The judges ruled the shot a dead ball due to interference and ordered her to start the frame all over again. Helen was so rattled by her airball that she only knocked down six pins in the frame.

* * *

During a 1966 league game, Agnes Kasner, of Portland, Oregon, tossed a ball that failed to reach the pins because of the intervention of Mother Nature. Seconds after Agnes released her ball, an earth tremor shook the bowling center with such force that the ball stopped three-quarters of the way down the lane! Agnes was allowed to reroll her ball.

Animal Crack-Ups

You see turkeys in bowling centers all the time, but rats and raccoons? Such critters have been known to make unwelcome appearances on the lanes.

During a league match at the Manhattan Lanes in New York in 1902, a bowler approached the line and fired his ball at a full rack. But to his amazement, all the pins toppled over before the ball ever reached them.

It was quickly discovered that a rat had scrambled out of a drain in the floor behind the lanes and scurried through the pins, knocking them all down.

"I thought the pins had fallen out of fear for my ball," said the bowler, who wanted to mark down a strike on his score sheet. The judge ordered him to rebowl the frame.

In 1934, a group of league bowlers in Dundee, New York, noticed that in the first two frames of their opening game, the head pin wobbled when it was set in place by the pinsetter. They soon figured out why.

In the third frame, rather than place the head pin, the pinsetter dropped a raccoon! Apparently, the curious creature had climbed into the machine during the night, shared space with the head pin, and was finally forced out by all the bowling action. After the raccoon fell, it waddled across the lanes and escaped out of an open window.

From Gutter to Glory

Pro Del Ballard, Jr., lost to Pete Weber in the nationally televised finals of the 1991 Fair Lanes Open in the most devastating way possible—with a gutter ball.

In the tourney at Randallstown, Maryland, Ballard needed two strikes and a seven in the tenth frame to beat Weber. Ballard drilled the first two strikes. A huge smile spread across his face as he sensed imminent victory. After all, how hard is it for a pro to knock down seven pins?

But Ballard made a critical error in strategy. Instead of safely rolling the ball down the middle for the seven, he tried to make his customary gutter-hugging hook. But Ballard slipped and put the ball in the channel.

Weber jumped out of his seat in disbelief while a stunned Ballard angrily stormed off the lane. The gutter ball cost him the title and $14,500—the difference between the $30,000 first-place prize and second-place money.

Once he cooled down, Ballard, to his credit, went along with the ribbing that followed his infamous roll. At a pro-am event the week after his misfire, Ballard rolled his first ball into the channel—on purpose. He received a standing ovation from the spectators.

At his next PBA Tour stop, the Long Island Open, Ballard was introduced to the crowd as "the guy who did something we'll never forget—and neither will he." Ballard laughed. Then he set out to show the world just how good a bowler he was.

In a semifinal match, he found himself in nearly the same situation he had been in in his game with Weber. Ballard needed a strike and an eight on his last two rolls for a win. He got the strike. The onlookers wondered if he would play it safe with a straight ball. Not a chance. Ballard went with his hook again and nailed another strike for a 250–247 win. Then he won the final match 223–183.

"I prayed I would get in a spot like that on TV again," he told the press afterward. "I'm thankful it came so soon. The title's the thing, but just rolling a big ball like that should erase all bad memories for me and hush the folks who had been kidding me."

Despite his statement, there was still one thing left for him to do before he could completely put that infamous gutter ball behind him. He got his chance in the finals of the 1993 King of the Hill competition when he wrapped up the title against his opponent, Pete Weber, with one ball to go in the tenth frame. On the last ball, Ballard deliberately threw it in the channel. Turning to the surprised spectators, he said, "I just wanted to prove I could throw a gutter ball and still beat Pete."

Bowled Over

Outrageous Achievements

First the Good News . . .

The good news was that Joe Wondra threw ten strikes.

The bad news was that he still failed to break 200.

Wondra, of St. Paul, Minnesota, achieved one of the freakiest scores ever in bowling history in 1914. Even though he racked up ten strikes, his final score was only 199!

Had he tossed just two more strikes, he would have rolled a perfect 300 game. Although it's hard to believe, the two strikes that he missed made a difference of a whopping 101 pins.

Here's how it happened:

Wondra started the game with three straight strikes. In the fourth frame, however, he knocked down only two pins on his first throw and just one pin on his second. That gave him a count of 68. Wondra then rolled a turkey, but botched up the eighth frame by knocking down three pins on his first ball and only one on his second. At the end of the eighth, his score was 139. Wondra then struck out on his next four balls to finish with a 199.

Substandard Bearer

The reputation of league bowler "Poodles" Nelson landed in the gutter in 1895—and has stayed there ever since.

Nelson bowled as part of the United Bowling Clubs of New York in the 1890s. Although he wasn't one of the better bowlers in the area, he loved the sport and became a charter member of the ABC in 1895.

That also happened to be the year he achieved ignoble immortality.

Nelson set an ABC season record that no one to this day has ever matched. While playing for the Defender Club of New York, Nelson rolled an unheard-of 89 gutter balls!

By setting the substandard in bad bowling, Nelson was given a special nickname by his fellow bowlers. Because many of them were born in Germany, they often used German terms when they bowled. The German slang word for throwing a gutter ball back then was "poodle."

So in honor of Nelson's horrendous number of gutter balls, they began calling him "Poodles"—a moniker that still lives in bowling infamy.

The Eleventh Hour

Like a new set of tenpins every frame, the number 11 kept cropping up for the Hippe bowling team of St. Louis in 1950.

In the schedule of the C.J.B. League, the Hippe's were team No. 11. In the 11th week of the league, the team won its 11th game on the 11th day of the 11th month. They were 11th in the standings, 11th in the high single-game standings, and 11th in the three-game series. The following week, they were scheduled to bowl on (what else?) Lane 11!

Warped Records

Bowlers have racked up some remarkable records—including ones that they wish everyone would forget. But these dubious marks have been etched for posterity in the ABC record book. Among the most warped records:

The biggest difference between a bowler's average and his worst score is held by George Stieber, of Detroit. Despite a 157 average, Stieber rolled a horrendous score during a Detroit Post Office League game in 1952. He shot an embarrassing 9—a whopping 148 points below his average!

* * *

Bud Mathieson, of Ocean Beach, California, was in a foul mood on December 30, 1946. He fouled fifteen times in a league game and thirty-seven times in the series that same night.

* * *

Mike Kappa, of Racine, Wisconsin, holds the league record for the lowest score ever—an ego-shattering 2! He was aided by eighteen gutters, one shy of the ABC mark of nineteen held by Richard Caplette, of Danielson, Connecticut, who notched a score of 3 in 1971.

* * *

The most possible splits in a game is eleven. Only one bowler has managed that futile feat in league play—Don Brayton, of Pawtucket, Rhode Island, in 1969. Payne Rose of St. Louis tossed six consecutive 7–10 splits in a 1962 match, while Virgil Distler, of Cincinnati threw four straight 5–7–10 splits in a 1974 game.

* * *

When it comes to a losing streak, no team has matched that of Downes Construction, of Moravia, New York. Between 1965 and 1967, the squad lost 120 straight league games!

Double Time

Identical twins Philip and Howard Hiob look alike, talk alike, and bowl alike. In fact, they finished the 1993 league season with identical averages—right down to a tenth of a pin!

The forty-seven-year-old brothers each rolled a 207.3 average for the year in the Wednesday Men's Commercial League in Alexandria, Virginia.

"I've never heard of anything like it," said Jerry Schneider, a spokesman for the ABC. "To our knowledge, that has never happened before in the history of the ABC."

* * *

Nancy Boynton and her twin sister Mary Lou Reed, of Columbia, South Dakota, bowled identical scores for all three games during the 1969 South Dakota WBA Tournament. While on the same team, they each rolled games of 190, 172, and 159 for a series total of 521.

* * *

At the tender age of seven, Scott and Matthew Higa, of San Francisco, became the youngest twins ever to bowl over 160 in a game.

In 1989, left-handed Scott scored a 166 while righty Matt rolled a 164.

The four-foot, fifty-pound twin strike force inherited their love for bowling from their parents Tom and Judy Higa, league regulars who began taking the boys to the alley at the age of two. The following year, the boys played in a tiny tots league and by age five, each had bowled his first 100-point game.

Said their mother, "One of their greatest pleasures is beating me on the lanes."

Toilet Bowl

Although Henry Beeny never made it into the Bowling Hall of Fame, he certainly qualified for the Bowling Hall of Shame.

In 1902, Beeny decided to compete in a major ABC tournament in Buffalo. With family and friends looking on, Beeny—who was a so-so bowler at best—completely fell apart on the lanes. Failing to pick up a single marker, he rolled a pitiful 59 in the opener. Things barely improved in his second game when he notched a woeful 63.

Try as he might to at least reach 100, Beeny couldn't even make it to 90, tallying only an 82. The total of his three-game series didn't match a decent game by an average pro. But his horrendous bowling did not go unnoticed by history.

Beeny made it into the record books. His total of 204 has remained, for over 90 years, the worst three-game series in ABC tournament history.

It should come as no surprise that Beeny ended up dead last in a field of 219 competitors—a full 153 points behind the 218th-place finisher!

Eight is Enough

Pro bowler Stan Kodish was stuck in a strange rut. He kept bowling the same score during the qualifying rounds of the 1988 PBA National Championships in Toledo, Ohio.

While rolling the identical scores in two or three consecutive games is not that unusual, Kodish bowled the same tally an unbelievable eight straight games! During one incredible stretch in the tourney, he kept tossing games of 202.

Even when he left the bowling center, he couldn't escape being haunted by that same number. When he returned to the hotel and got out his room key, Kodish suddenly realized that the number to his room was none other than 202!

Thinking that maybe he was caught in the clutches of some mystical numerological phenomenon, Kodish returned to the front desk. "I figured that the room number had something to do with my scores, so I asked if Room 300 was available," he recalled. "Unfortunately, it wasn't."

Despite his amazing string of 202s, Kodish failed to make the cut. If only he had made a reservation for Room 300 . . .

Fit to Be Tied

The teams from Behrens Metalware and Rothers Appliance knew they were evenly matched, but they had no idea just how evenly.

During their league match in 1938 in Wautoma, Wisconsin, Behrens Metalware squeaked by Rothers Appliance 883–876 in the first game. Rothers came back in the second match, winning by the same seven-point margin, 853–846.

Now the teams squared off for their third and final game to determine the winner. Amazingly, the contest ended in a 866 deadlock.

But what was even more incredible, Behrens and Rothers

tied the series! Both teams rolled a total score of 2,595 each. According to the ABC, it was the first and only time a league series ever ended in a tie.

* * *

How's this for a well-balanced team? All five men on the Peoria Bowl Recreation team in Peoria, Illinois, ended the 1949–1950 season with the exact same average—180.

It's happened twice since then. Each of the five members of the Oberle Trailers team of Syracuse, New York, rolled 167 during the 1960–1961 season while the quintet from Pete's Bait Shop in Joliet, Illinois, each averaged 171 in the 1985–1986 season.

* * *

During a league game in 1987, all five members of Kilmer's Flagstone team of Clarks Summit, Pennsylvania, shot the identical score of 201.

Two other teams have accomplished that feat. Each member of Moffat's Ale of Syracuse, New York, and Coors, of Miami, Arizona, rolled 192, respectively, in 1936 and 1962.

In 1978, Don Johnson was given the Steve Nagy Memorial Award for being the nicest guy on the PBA Tour. In his acceptance speech, he noted that years earlier, when he was winning, he wasn't all that popular among his fellow bowlers. "Now that I'm bowling badly," he said, "I've got lots of friends."

Bowling for Dollars

No bowling TV show delivered more drama and laughs than "Jackpot Bowling."

Debuting in 1959, the show featured two bowlers who rolled nine balls each. The man with the most strikes won $1,000 and returned the following week, while the loser went home with $250. A bowler who strung together six strikes in a row earned $5,000. If nobody threw a double turkey, the kitty would build by $1,000 each week until someone hit it.

Don Carter became the first to roll six straight strikes. But the biggest stir in the show's inaugural year was caused by Andy Varipapa who, at the age of sixty-eight, became the first and only bowler on "Jackpot Bowling" to roll all nine strikes.

In the show's second year, Frank Clause, a middle-aged schoolteacher who bowled in many tournaments but never struck it big, captured the hearts of the viewing audience. Gunning for the jackpot, Clause threw five consecutive strikes but was tapped on the sixth. A few days later, he received a bill from a fan of the show. The viewer claimed he had become so excited when Clause's lone pin refused to fall that he kicked over his television set and wanted the bowler to pay for it.

Clause, who remained on the show for nine weeks before he was defeated, finally rolled six straight strikes and won the jackpot, which had grown to $26,000.

In its third year, the show, which was sponsored by Phillies Cigars, was hosted by funnyman Milton Berle and featured a jackpot kitty that grew $5,000 per week and a double turkey worth $25,000. Celebrity guests also got the chance to roll a ball for charity.

Comedian Buddy Hackett had viewers in stitches when he showed up with two bowling balls attached to both ends of a forty-two-inch-wide pole. Hackett intended to roll the balls in the lane's two gutters and sweep the deck with the pole. But the balls became stuck in the channel and Hackett's contraption knocked down only the head pin.

Of all the shows, none was more talked about than the night Therman "Roly Poly" Gibson took home the biggest booty ever on "Jackpot Bowling." The five-foot-ten, 240-pound Detroit bowler, who later was inducted into the ABC Hall of Fame, had a fluid delivery and a keen eye for the pins.

On January 2, 1961, he rolled six consecutive strikes and claimed the jackpot—a whopping $75,000. Berle was so shocked he was speechless as he hugged Gibson. But the feat turned bitter-sweet for the kegler the next year at tax time.

According to *Bowlers Journal International,* "Gibson just plain forgot to tell his tax preparer about the $75,000 booty when they were working on his tax report for 1961. It never occurred to him that in Detroit, the world's number one bowling city, every IRS agent not only was likely to be a bowler, but had been watching as a fellow named Therman Gibson was making bowling history!"

Racking Up Records

Bowlers are always trying to find novel ways to set records. Among the most outrageous marks are:

Most pins knocked down in twenty-four hours:
37,827—Mike Cernobyl, West Palm Beach, Florida, 1989

Cernobyl knocked down 37,827 pins in a grueling, twenty-four-hour marathon. He rolled 203 games—one every seven minutes—ad averaged an amazing 186 during the day-and-night effort.

Even more remarkable, he shot better near the end of the marathon than he did when he first started. He bowled a 233 in his 193rd game and a 223 in his 200th game.

* * *

Most games bowled in a week:
1,050 games—Gus Garrido, Tampa, Florida, 1965

Garrido bowled more games in a week than most bowlers do in years.

He bowled almost continuously during his week-long marathon, stopping briefly only for food, catnaps, and much-needed massages. During his bowlathon, which lasted an exhausting 164 hours and 22 minutes, Garrido lifted a total of 270,144 pounds of weight, threw 19,296 times with a fourteen-pound ball, knocked down 152,437 pins, and walked 109.63 miles on his approach. His highest game was 289 and his lowest was 45.

Garrido broke the old record of 1,042 games in 183 hours and 33 minutes, set by Jim Hartley in 1960.

* * *

Most bowling balls stacked one on top of one another:
9 balls—Dave Kremer, St. Louis, 1988

"A bunch of us were standing around the bowling alley one night after a few beers and one guy said he knew someone who could stack three bowling balls on top of each other," Kremer recalled. "Another guy said he saw someone stack four. I told them, 'I bet I can balance more than that.'" Moments later, he successfully stacked seven. It took him another couple of months before he could stack nine—a feat recorded on videotape by a local TV crew.

His secret? "I always place the thumbhole of the first ball down, which steadies it," Kremer explained. "The next thumbhole will go on top of the center of the first ball. There's a weight between the thumb and finger holes, so the thumbholes are always down." He sets heavy sixteen-pound balls at the bottom, progresses to the fourteen- and twelve-pound balls, and tops it off with eight-pounders.

* * *

Most weight lost bowling in one day:
12 pounds—Joe Kester, Portage, Wisconsin, 1938

Kester, manager of the Hotel Raulf bowling alley, wanted to prove to people that bowling was good exercise. He announced that he would bowl 100 games in one day with the condition that he would bowl an extra game every time he scored less than 125.

That morning, Kester weighed in at 170 pounds. Sixteen hours and 101 games later, he stepped on the scale. He now weighed 158 pounds—a twelve-pound loss. Kester may have proved his point, but he needed four days to recuperate.

* * *

Longest distance a bowling ball has been thrown by a pro:
14,000 feet—Steve Nagy, Colorado, 1953

On an exhibition tour in Colorado, Nagy tossed the ball for a longer distance than any other pro. He hurled his ball from the summit of Pike's Peak.

When Rita Jones appeared in an Indianapolis court for a speeding violation in 1965, Judge John L. McNelis asked her, "Where were you going in such a hurry?"

"Bowling," she replied.

"What's your highest score?" he asked.

"265."

"Beats mine," said the judge. "Case dismissed."

Alley Oops!

Mindless Mishaps

Tapped Out

A kegler was once knocked out by his own ball!

It happened in 1962 in Toledo after Leonard Konieczny complained to the manager of the bowling center that the pinspotting machine had caused a four-inch scratch on his favorite ball.

"My ball is cracked," he told the manager. "And even if it isn't cracked right at this moment, this scratch is bad enough to develop a crack. I want a new ball."

The manager tried to convince the bowler that there was nothing wrong with the ball. To prove his point, the manager bounced Konieczny's ball several times on the asphalt tile floor. Each time, the ball rebounded into his hands. "If the ball was cracked, it wouldn't have bounced back into my hands like that," the manager told the bowler. "It would be dead and have a flat sound."

Still not convinced, Konieczny thought the ball needed a better test than on asphalt tile. So he decided to bounce his ball on the concrete sidewalk outside. Taking the ball in both hands, Konieczny slammed it onto the sidewalk. The ball hit with a loud wham. Then it shot back up—and smacked the bowler right under the chin. Konieczny crumpled to the sidewalk, kayoed by his own ball.

When Konieczny was revived a few minutes later, he heard one unsympathetic bystander tell another, "Looks like he was tapped but good!"

Sole Man

Frank Bruno would have bowled otherwise unnoticed at the 1915 National Bowling Association championships if he hadn't become a victim of what was described at the time as "one of the most bizarre injuries in the history of organized American tenpins."

Bruno, of Onawa, British Columbia, was bowling in the fourth frame of his second game in the singles competition at New York's Grand Central Palace. As he was about to release the ball, he slid his right foot toward the foul line and let out a yelp. A sliver of maple from the approach ripped through the buckskin sole of his right shoe and tore into his foot.

Wincing in pain, Bruno lost his balance and sprawled about ten feet past the foul line. Meanwhile, he inadvertently launched his sixteen-pound ball high into the air. The ball then crashed back onto the lane just inches from Bruno's head.

As the stunned and injured bowler sat up on the lane, he heard the cold-hearted referee whistle a foul.

With the splinter still lodged in his foot, Bruno limped back to the settee. Then, gritting his teeth, he pulled a four-inch sliver out from the bottom of his bloody foot. Not only did his foot hurt but so did his thumb, which was badly sprained from falling on it when he took his spill.

Bruno told the officials he couldn't continue and requested that his game be temporarily suspended until he had mended. After considerable discussion, the officials agreed to let him return two days later to pick up where he had left off.

Bruno then hobbled off to the drugstore for iodine to treat his wound. After a much needed rest, he resumed his game, but failed to finish among the leaders.

Wrecking Balls

Bowling balls don't always roll down the alley. They've been known to take some strange paths that have caused havoc for their owners.

In 1960, Louie Montesi, of Memphis, had just purchased a new ball and was driving to the bowling center to try it out for the first time. Stopping for a red light, Montesi heard a thump outside his car and then an "oh-oh" from his thirteen-year-old son in the backseat.

The boy had been playing with the ball when he accidentally pitched it out the open window. It was just Montesi's luck that the error in judgment happened at the top of a hill. As cars swerved to avoid the runaway object, the ball rolled merrily down the street and into a sewer drain two blocks away.

Montesi needed the help of the Memphis Sewer Department to retrieve what in every sense of the term was his gutter ball.

* * *

In Syracuse in 1958, an unnamed woman bowler boarded a bus and headed for the bowling alley. She placed her bowling bag, which had a broken zipper and wouldn't close, on the floor.

Moments later, when the traffic light turned red, the bus driver slammed on his brakes. The sudden stop caused the bowling bag to tip over, and the ball rolled out of the bag and down the aisle.

A drunken passenger took one look at the ball and shouted, "It's a bomb! Run!" The other passengers screamed in panic and dashed off the bus before the chagrined bowler had a chance to tell everyone it was just a bowling ball.

* * *

William R. Williams discovered that a bowling ball can do more than knock down pins. It can trigger an embarrassing traffic accident.

In 1976, Williams, thirty-nine, of Wilkes-Barre, Pennsylvania, was driving with his trusty bowling ball by his side on the front seat. As he neared a stop sign, he applied the brakes a little too hard, causing his ball to roll off the seat and drop onto the accelerator.

The car sped up, startling Williams so much that he lost control of his vehicle. His auto smashed into a parked car and the impact pushed the struck car into another parked vehicle. Williams escaped injury, but not the memory of a car crash caused by his bowling ball.

* * *

A bowling ball can cause a headache, as a policeman in Elgin, Illinois, found out in 1992.

Responding to a complaint about a noisy tenant, Officer Brian Gorcowski was climbing the stairs leading to the suspect's second-floor apartment when someone flicked off the stairwell light. Suddenly, the policeman was bonked on the head by a sixteen-pound bowling ball that had been dropped from the second-floor landing.

Despite minor cuts and bruises—and a splitting headache—Officer Gorcowski arrested the suspect on charges of aggravated battery. The bowling ball was taken to the police station as evidence.

* * *

In 1961, Louisa Murray was sitting at a table at an outdoor café in Burlington, Vermont, minding her own business, when she was kayoed by a bowling ball.

The ball had rolled off the table and out an open window of a third-floor apartment above the restaurant. The falling ball glanced off Louisa's head and smashed into her wrist. The young woman was rushed to the hospital with a head injury.

Fortunately, Louisa recovered and discovered that some good had come from the mishap. When the ball struck her wrist, it broke the crystal of her Timex, but the watch kept ticking. Back then, Timex was running an ad campaign extolling the sturdiness and dependability of its watches. When its ad agency learned about Louisa's accident with the flying bowling ball and that her watch still worked, the agency hired her to appear in an ad.

Louisa became a model for the watch company, offering her watch as proof that Timex "takes a lickin' and keeps on tickin'."

Leaving One Standing

During one memorable trip to a tournament, Walter Ray Williams, Jr., Bowler of the Year in 1986, felt like a lone pin left standing.

In 1988, he and his girlfriend Paige Pennington were driving in his van from the Miller Lite Championship in Milwaukee (where he finished thirty-eighth) to the Fair Lanes Open in Baltimore. With Williams sleeping in the back in the wee hours of the morning, Paige pulled into a turnpike rest area to use the bathroom.

"I woke up, got out of the van, and went to the men's room," Williams recalled. "When I came back, she was gone. Obviously she didn't know she had left me. The blankets in the back were over the pillows and she thought it was me."

The bowler called turnpike officials to tell them his girlfriend accidentally had left him behind and he asked if they would flag her down. But they wouldn't do it.

Paige drove another 100 miles before stopping at another rest area to use the bathroom again. "By this time, she was getting a little mad because she wanted me to drive," Williams said. "She had begun to wonder if I was ever going to wake up."

The bowler called turnpike officials again and gave them a description of the van. It just so happened Paige had arrived at the toll booth moments after the toll collector had received the van's description.

"He asked her if her name was Paige," said Williams. "When she told him yes, he asked her if she had forgotten something. She said no. Then he asked if she had forgotten *someone*. She looked in the back of the van and called out 'Walter Ray? Walter Ray?' The toll collector told her I was back at the last rest area. Paige thought he meant the last one where she had just stopped. When she returned and I wasn't there, she started to panic. She didn't know what had happened to me.

"Paige called her mother in California. When her mother answered, Paige said, 'Oh, Mom, I've lost Walter Ray!' Her mother laughed and told her I was at the first rest area. I had called a lot of people that day, including her mother. I was stranded there for five hours with nothing except a telephone. What else could I do?"

Williams could have saved himself the trouble of driving to Baltimore. He failed to cash in at the Fair Lanes Open.

Once when pro bowler Carmen Salvino fell into a slump, he took some time off to study film of his earlier days. When he returned to the tour, one of his fellow bowlers asked him if he noticed anything from the films. "Yes," said Salvino. "I noticed I'm losing more hair."

The Eagle Has (Crash) Landed

It took Pete Weber fifty-six grueling games and eight days to win the 1991 U.S. Open Championship. But it took him only a few seconds to lose the coveted trophy.

No one gave Weber much of a chance of capturing the championship. He was in fifty-eighth place when the 240-man field was trimmed down to sixty, and he brought up the rear when the field was cut to twenty-four for the match play.

Averaging 220, Weber won fifteen games in the round-robin tournament and climbed to fifth place to reach the finals. Then he whipped each of his four opponents to capture the title, the $40,000 first-place prize money, and the trophy—a hand-crafted, porcelain bald eagle.

At a photographer's request, Weber hoisted the trophy over his head. To everyone's shock, the eagle promptly fell off its walnut base, to which it had been glued. The eagle took a swan dive, crashed to the lane, and shattered into hundreds of pieces.

Fans poured out of the stands, fell to their knees and scuffled for fragments as keepsakes. One of the souvenir hunters was Pete's dad, Hall of Famer Dick Weber. He walked off with a big chunk of the eagle's wing.

An embarrassed Wally Hall, president of the Bowling Proprietors Association of America, which sponsored the tournament, promised Weber the smashed eagle would be replaced. Sighed Weber, "At least I still have the base."

Picture Imperfect

The 1904 ABC National Championships gave birth to a tournament superstition that is still followed by many bowling teams to this day.

During the event, which was held in Cleveland, the team from Barberton, Ohio, rolled two exceptional games that vaulted the squad into first place. The Barberton bowlers felt cocky and were convinced they had the team title cinched, even though there was still one more game to go.

Because they wanted to get their picture into the early editions of the morning paper, the team stopped bowling in the fifth frame of the last game to pose for a photograph. That turned out to be a big mistake.

When they returned to bowling, the Barberton team couldn't buy a strike or a spare over the final five frames. With their bravado wilting away with each open frame, the Barberton bowlers finished fifth in the standings.

Since that night, according to legend, no serious bowling team considers having its picture taken before or during tournament games.

The Old (Bowling) Ball and Chain

When it came to poking fun at marriage, bridegroom Dan Herr dropped the ball. In this case, it was a bowling ball—and it landed on the bride's foot.

"We're both pretty red-faced about what happened," Dan told reporters.

The wedding between Dan and his bride Lisa went off without a hitch in Port Washington, Wisconsin, in 1990. At the reception, Dan decided to joke about the loss of his freedom by carrying around a fifteen-pound bowling ball that was chained to his ankle.

"I was supposed to sing a song, telling Lisa to take the ball and chain away," Dan said. "Instead, she ended up singing the blues."

While the couple took a spin on the dance floor, Dan held the bowling ball in one arm and his lovely new bride in the other. Suddenly, the ball slipped from his grasp and landed on Lisa's foot.

When an ice pack failed to stop her pain, she was taken to the emergency room, where she was treated for a fractured toe. "We laugh about it now," said Lisa, who was forced to start her married life on crutches decorated with ribbons from the wedding reception.

"Everything is fine now and we're real happy," added Dan. "We just got off on the wrong foot."

By Hook or By Crook

Law-Breaking Bowlers

In the Fast Lane

A funny thing happened to pro bowler Mike Neumann on his way to winning the $100,000 first-place prize at the 1991 Hoinke Super Classic. He landed in jail.

Neumann and fellow pro Brian Eaton decided to drive together in Neumann's car from their hometown of Niagara Falls, New York, to Cincinnati, where the tourney was being held. But on the way, with Eaton behind the wheel, they got nailed by a small-town Ohio policeman who clocked them going well over the speed limit. When a check of Neumann's auto registration revealed some unpaid speeding tickets, his car was impounded and both bowlers were tossed into the slammer.

Neumann was allowed one phone call. So he called pro bowler Craig Woodhouse, who was just leaving for the Hoinke Super Classic. Woodhouse stopped by on his way to the tourney, bailed out the locked-up bowlers, and drove them the rest of the way to the event.

Worried about how they would get back home, Neumann and Eaton made a deal that if either won, they'd fly back home, with the winner picking up the tab.

The jailhouse experience did nothing to slow down Neumann's powerhouse ball. Neumann, who averaged 234 throughout his eleven matches, won the title match convincingly, 277–217, and pocketed $100,000.

"Don't worry about getting your car back," said one of his fellow competitors. "With the money you just won, you can buy a new car. Heck, you can buy four new ones!"

During a nationwide tour in 1940, famed trick-shot artist Andy Varipapa met two priests who had seen him perform three nights in a row. They told him they were planning to attend his next performance in another town. One of the priests asked Varipapa, "We noticed that your show is always the same. Are you planning to do any new trick shots at your next show?" Replied Varipapa, "Father, when you go to a different town, do you change the prayers?"

A Perfect Excuse

High school senior Ray Williams was reading the lanes when he should have been reading his textbooks.

In a special promotion in 1993, Miracle Lanes in Monroeville, Pennsylvania, offered free bowling from 5 A.M. to 9 A.M. and a $1,000 prize to any bowler who rolled a 300 game.

Hundreds of bowlers showed up, including some who lined up outside the center as early as 4 A.M. Twenty-five minutes before the promotion expired, Williams, eighteen, rolled his twelfth consecutive strike for a perfect game to earn the thousand bucks and the cheers and applause of the crowd. Because the event, known as the Inaugural Bowl, drew lots of media attention, Williams gave several interviews after his perfect game. His live interview on a local radio station was heard by avid listeners throughout the area—including the principal of his school.

The principal called up Williams to congratulate him on his feat—and then reminded the student that he had been bowling when he should have been in school. Because of his unauthorized absence, Williams was given four days of detention for playing hooky.

Said Williams, "It was worth it."

35

Bowling's Most Wanted

Amanda Guild bowled so well in league competition that she got her picture in the paper. Most everyone in town saw the photo—including law enforcement officials who had been looking for her.

In 1990, the thirty-year-old mother and avid bowler was playing in a tournament at the American Lanes in Buena Vista near Saginaw, Michigan. Though her league average was only 131, Amanda caught fire and rolled a 160, then a 203, and finally an impressive 224. Her series of 587 gave her an average of 196—a whopping 65 pins higher than her league average.

Amanda's performance earned her the honor of "Bowler of the Week" which included a story and photo of her in the *Saginaw News.*

And it was that picture which eventually led to her arrest. The photo caught the eye of a U.S. marshal who was glancing through the paper.

Friends on Amanda's bowling team thought she was just one of the girls. But it turned out that she was wanted by federal authorities for her role in a major interstate money laundering and drug trafficking operation in Michigan, Tennessee, and Texas.

"Amanda had been indicted along with five other suspects in the ring," said Steven Kurkowski, a deputy U.S. marshal. "We'd been looking for her for months. The others had been arrested, but we couldn't find her anywhere."

Amanda had fled from Tennessee to her hometown of Saginaw, but her whereabouts remained unknown until the chance sighting in the newspaper.

"If I was wanted by the police, I certainly wouldn't want my picture in the paper," said Kurkowski.

Authorities decided to apprehend Amanda the following week at the scene of her fame—the bowling center. "We could have arrested her at home," said Kurkowski. "But since she was Bowler of the Week, what could be more appropriate than to nab her at the bowling alley?

"She was in the fourth frame of her first game when we arrived. I showed her my badge and all she said was, 'Can we get out of here?'

"When she went to her preliminary hearing the next morning, she was still wearing her bowling shirt with the little pin attached that said 'Bowler of the Week.' She went from Bowler of the Week to Arrest of the Week."

When a Detroit area bowler rolled a 700 series in a local tournament in 1966, a reporter asked his name.

"Perry Como," responded the bowler.

"Hey, that's quite a well-known name," said the reporter.

"It darn well ought to be. I've been bowling in this league for ten years."

All Bets Are Off

Five Los Angeles housewives plunked $7.50 in pocket change into a kitty during their weekly league bowling match, to be claimed by the one who rolled the highest score.

Then they started bowling—and all hell broke loose.

Incredibly, vice cops who had staked out the bowling center busted the stunned homemakers for betting on bowling! The women were given a gambling citation which carried a fine of up to $1,000.

"We were totally in shock," declared bowler Anne Barnett following her arrest in 1990. "We are all law-abiding citizens who have a penny-ante bet on our game each week to provide a little bit of extra excitement.

"It's literally nickels and dimes in our pot, yet we were treated like big-time criminals. I couldn't believe the cops could be so petty and stupid!"

Said bowling buddy Sandy Scholnick, who was also nabbed in the roundup, "Aren't there more important things for police to do than sit in a bowling alley all morning, watching a bunch of housewives bowl and bet a few dollars? What a waste of taxpayers' money!"

Other members of the bowling league were outraged when they saw police making the arrests, said Barnett. "One lady demanded their badge numbers and yelled, 'Don't you guys know there's a high school down the block where drugs are sold on campus? Why don't you stop harassing these women and start earning your money?' The cops yelled back and it was total pandemonium."

When word of the arrests got back to headquarters, red-faced police officials quickly dispatched officers to the homes of the five women and retrieved the citations. All of the charges were dropped.

Admitted a police administrator, "I think we went a little bit overboard."

Suit Yourself

Rather than wait for the courts to resolve a lawsuit, the two adversaries decided to settle it on the lanes.

In New York in 1904, Fred Anderson sued his former business partner, Edward Underhill, for $1,138 in a dispute over some office furniture. Because of a backlog in the court dockets, both parties were told the suit might not be resolved for a long time.

A few days later, Anderson was having lunch with his attorney in a building that also housed a bowling alley. Anderson, an avid bowler, challenged his lawyer to a game.

But before they started, they bumped into Underhill and his attorney. Underhill, who also fancied himself as a good bowler, came up with a proposal for Anderson: "Look, rather than have this case drag out in court, let's get it settled right now. I will play you the best two out of three games. If I win, I owe you nothing. If you win, I will pay your claim."

"That's fine with me," said Anderson, taking off his coat and rolling up his sleeves. "Let's get started."

With their attorneys acting as scorekeepers, the two bowlers battled it out. Underhill won the first game, 171 to 153, but Anderson stormed back to capture the second contest, 204 to 160. Then he polished off Underhill in the rubber match, 170 to 156.

Declared an extremely happy Anderson, "Judgment in favor of the plaintiff!"

Split Personalities

Nutty Characters

The Hustlers' Hustler

John "The Count" Gengler was bowling's most notorious hustler.

To Gengler, life was just a bowl of cherries. And the cherries were local keglers whose pockets he emptied with skill and cunning.

Born in Luxembourg in 1887, the tall, slender hustler spoke with a thick accent. He dressed in elegant attire and had a stiff regal bearing that gave people the impression he was a foreign diplomat or an international banker—anything but a bowler. He wasn't just a good bowler; he was a great one. Gengler could put a ball anywhere he wanted most every time.

In 1915, he showed up in Schenectady, New York, where he displayed the modus operandi he would use for years throughout the United States.

The Count strode into the bowling alley with his opera cloak whirling around him, a black satin top hat on his head. Tapping the lane with his cane, he asked the local bowlers, "What's this for? Dancing?"

The rubes laughed. Gengler took a seat, strictly as a

spectator, as the area's best bowlers engaged in $50 pot games in which gamblers made book. Eventually, Gengler struck up a conversation with the bowlers and asked to join in the match.

"I used to play ninepins in Germany, but I bet I can play this game," he said. "Mind if I get in?" Figuring he was an easy mark, the bowlers welcomed him—and his money.

Gengler peeled off his coat but kept on his tie and vest. Then he selected a house ball and took off his shoes. Standing three feet from the foul line in his stockings, he took one long step forward with his left foot and threw the ball with his palm without using the finger holes.

Despite his weird bowling form, the nattily dressed stranger managed a few strikes and spares in the game and expressed satisfaction with his performance even though he was badly beaten. He bet again and lost, only this time by a much smaller margin. Then he won, but just barely. Finally, he set the trap.

"I knew I could play this game," the Count declared. "This is even easier with ten pins. Anyone want to bowl for $100 a game?" The best money bowler stepped forward and Gengler covered all bets until $1,000 was riding on the next game. The Count won, but only by a few pins. So they agreed to a rematch. And Gengler won again . . . and again. He cleaned out the house—the bowler, the backers, and the bettors—and then swept off into the night.

Gengler crisscrossed the country from New York to California. He stayed at the best hotels and dressed as if he was on the boulevards of Paris. Bowling news didn't travel very fast in those days, so few local hotshots were aware of his special skills. In town after town, the locals would wait in line to bowl Gengler and they would leave broke. The Count never cheated; he conned people into wagers. He bet his own money and bowled against the best, beating them on their own lanes.

Eventually, Gengler was exposed as a hustler by an Omaha sportswriter who had seen the Count divest several Nebraska bowlers of their money. The reporter wrote a story entitled, "Beware the Count" for Chicago's *Bowling Journal*.

When Gengler breezed into the Windy City, his cover was blown. But surprisingly, bowlers still challenged him. Not surprisingly, they still lost.

"I had no trouble in lining up matches in New York," Gengler recalled years later. "That's where I picked up my nickname. A pinboy, seeing my cane, figured I must be visiting nobility and pinned it on me. The nickname really stuck when a bowler asked why I was called the Count and someone said, 'That's because, after each match, he's the one counting the money.'"

The key to Gengler's success was his preparation before a match. He carefully studied the surface of each lane and the action of his opponent's ball.

Once, for a high stakes match at a place where he had never bowled before, Gengler cleverly sidestepped a ground rule that no practice was allowed. A few days before the match, Gengler hired a pinboy to throw ball after ball down the alleys. The Count made notes. "I even went down to the pits to watch the pin action," he recalled. By the time the match started, Gengler knew the lanes better than his opponent did and easily won.

Eventually, only the foolhardy dared challenge the Count to a money match, so he began staging exhibitions before huge, appreciative crowds.

But because of his notoriety as a hustler, Gengler was banned from ABC tournaments. To this day, bowling's most infamous character has yet to be installed in the ABC Hall of Fame.

A Flair for the Dramatic

For sheer contrived drama, no one could match ABC Hall of Famer Paul Krumske.

Voted Chicago's "Bowler of the Half Century" in 1951, Krumske would go to any length to heighten the suspense of a match just to unnerve his opponent—including faking a heart attack.

Once, during a tense match with fellow Hall of Famer Ned Day, Krumske stopped in the middle of a game that he was losing. He excused himself, staggered into the men's room, and started groaning as if he was going to die. "Poor Ned, gentle soul that he was, became so upset that when the match resumed, his strikes became few and far between," recalled Carmen Salvino.

Another time, when his Meister Brau team from Chicago was getting whipped by the Pfieffer Beer team from Detroit, Krumske whispered to his teammates, "No matter what I do, don't let it bother you." Then he stood up, grabbed his chest, and collapsed on the lane.

Everyone huddled around the stricken bowler. By the time the ambulance arrived fifteen minutes later, Krumske was sitting up. He took some oxygen and then announced that he was feeling much better—so good, in fact, that he would continue bowling. "It's just my old heart condition," he told everyone. "I'm much better now. Let's bowl."

Krumske then proceeded to throw a strike. The half-hour interruption turned the tide for his team. The Pfieffers, slightly shaken by the incident, never got back in their groove. Instead, the Meister Braus, with Krumske leading the way, stormed back to win the match.

Krumske's flair for the dramatic often was aimed at tweaking his own teammates.

When Salvino bowled on Krumske's Meister Brau team, which won a couple of Chicago League titles, Salvino often felt like strangling his teammate. "Krumske was so good that I'd swear he'd bowl poorly sometimes just so he could make a dramatic comeback," Salvino recalled.

"Once in a team match, I got mad at him after he had fooled around for nine frames and then struck out in the tenth to give us a one-pin win. 'If you'd have bowled better before, you would have saved us a lot of stress and strain,' I said. Krumske gave me a disgusted look. 'Damn it, kid, we won, didn't we?' he snapped. 'You don't appreciate nothin'.'

"I'd much rather bowl with him than against him, if only because he was one of the most fidgety bowlers who ever lived," said Salvino.

Krumske had this annoying habit of rubbing his right hand up and down his pant leg before he threw. He did it so often he would drive opponents as well as spectators crazy.

One time during a title match, Krumske needed a strike to clinch the game in the tenth frame. The tension mounted as Krumske stood on the approach and rubbed his hand on his pants for several minutes. Finally, a woman in the bleachers couldn't stand it anymore and began counting out loud for everyone to hear, "34 . . . 35 . . . 36 . . . Throw the ball already!"

Krumske stopped rubbing, turned around, glowered at the spectator, and then resumed his rubbing. An interminable two minutes later, he rolled the ball—and got his strike.

"Lady," he said after the pins dropped, "that was for you."

Dressed for Success

No hustler was more outlandish in the 1960s than Ernie Schlegel.

Dressed in outrageous clothes, Schlegel conned easy marks into thinking he was a lousy, drunken bowler and then cleaned out their wallets.

But Schlegel eventually cleaned up his act, became a five-time winner on the pro circuit, and was even elected president of the PBA in 1987 and 1988.

Schlegel was a problem kid while growing up in Manhattan. At Bronx Vocational High School, he flouted school regulations. "We were supposed to wear ties," he recalled in a *Sports Illustrated* interview. "I hate ties. So I'd buy shoestring licorice, knot it together, and wear it around my neck. Then I'd eat my necktie in class."

When he was ordered by the principal to take part in an extracurricular activity of his choosing, Schlegel joined the school's bowling team. He quickly realized he was a natural-born bowler and became remarkably good at it.

After graduation in 1960, Schlegel worked as a stock boy for a watch manufacturer during the day for $50 a week. But at night, he would hustle at the lanes around town for up to $500 a game.

"I'd bowl all weekend and get back just in time Monday morning to go to work," he said. "After about six weeks of this, I was so tired I literally fell asleep on my feet one day. The boss tapped me on the shoulder and before he could say anything, I said, 'Forget it. I quit.' That night I showed my parents the dresser drawer where I kept my winnings. It was filled with stacks and stacks of money, thousands of dollars. I didn't trust banks. My parents let me quit the job as a stock boy."

Schlegel began hustling full time. No one could miss spotting him. He often dressed in black stovepipe pants, a white silk shirt, an iridescent raincoat, and high Roman heels. He also sported a Mohican haircut and carried an umbrella with its tip filed to a point for protection on the city's mean streets.

He once used that umbrella when it wasn't raining. Schlegel went to collect on a $150 wager that he had won, but the loser shoved him through a plate glass window. So Schlegel got up and retaliated with his umbrella. He was indicted for attempted murder, but was acquitted.

With his legal problems out of the way, Schlegel went on a two-year hustling streak in which he hardly lost a match. His best night netted him $7,500.

His trick in winning, besides being a super bowler, was his act. "Before I bowled, I'd have one drink and throw a shot of bourbon on my head or down my neck," he recalled. "That way, when I got to the bowling center, I smelled real good. Then I'd bowl guys who were sure I was drunk. I crushed them. After a while, though, everybody knew me, and my hustling days ended."

Eventually, Schlegel straightened up and joined the PBA in 1968 at the age of twenty-five. He immediately made his mark on the pro circuit, not so much for his bowling (he didn't win a tournament until 1980), but for his clothes. He became the flashiest dresser on the tour. Wearing bright sequin-decorated outfits in red, white, and blue, Schlegel stood out from the rest of the pros. Because of his penchant for the patriotic colors, Schlegel was given a nickname by his fellow bowlers: "U.S.A."

The Masked Marvel

He was a member of a championship team, voted Bowler of the Year in 1942, and inducted into the ABC Hall of Fame.

But hustler and pro bowler Johnny Crimmins achieved far greater fame as his alter ego, the Masked Marvel.

From the 1920s through the 1940s, the Detroit-born kegler would don a mask and bowl the local hotshots throughout the Midwest for cash.

"When I first started bowling, I couldn't hit the ground with a ball," he recalled. "I was really bad. But I was hooked on the game, and kept going. Fifteen years and a hell of a lot of lines later, I developed my instinct for the game. I also had a 213 average."

Crimmins joined Joe Norris's Strohs team, where he earned his moniker as "The General" for his take-charge attitude. A bowler with a fierce competitive streak, Crimmins loved to psych out opponents. Often he would go up to a bowler and say, "You've changed your delivery slightly since I last saw you, haven't you?" The opponent would wonder what little change Crimmins was talking about, lose his concentration, and then the game.

As much as Crimmins loved bowling on a team, he made far more money hustling from Chicago to Cleveland as the Masked Marvel. Attired in a black hood with holes cut out for his eyes, nose, and mouth, he would swoop into a bowling center and announce, "I am the Masked Marvel. Who thinks he's man enough to beat me?"

At first, bowlers, not knowing who he was, would line up for a chance to knock off the hooded character. More often than not, they left the lanes with a much lighter wallet.

It didn't take long for his cover to get blown. Ironically, few people knew what Crimmins looked like, but everyone knew who the Masked Marvel was—and they didn't want to bowl against him. "Whenever I cased a joint to bowl in, nobody recognized me without my mask on," Crimmins recalled. "But the second I tossed that thing on and came stomping in, everybody cleared out. I had to practically harass people for matches."

Added Norris, "If he just had walked into a place without his hood, nobody would have known who he was and he could have had some money games."

The Fairest of Them All

Hustler Marie Warmbier loved nothing better than to beat male bowlers who thought women were the weaker sex.

Warmbier, who posthumously became a charter member of the Women's International Bowling Congress Hall of Fame in 1953, plied her trade during the 1920s and 1930s before she died at the age of thirty-nine. A noted exhibition player, Warmbier toured 16,000 miles for the Bowling Proprietors Association of America in 1935, winning over 400 matches against each area's top male bowlers.

A woman with steel nerves and a fiery temperament, Warmbier would take on most any challenge and play for money. One time, Louie Petersen, owner of Warmbier's favorite bowling establishment in her hometown of Chicago, received a boastful letter from a proprietor in Wichita. The letter claimed there were a dozen women in Wichita who were better bowlers than Warmbier.

Warmbier was furious and traveled to Wichita, where she confronted the letter-writer. Plunking down five $100 bills on the counter of his bowling alley, Warmbier declared, "Here is $500 that says no woman here can beat me in a ten-game match."

The owner gulped and refused to take the bet. However, he proposed that she take on three of his best male bowlers. Warmbier's eyes lit up and she readily agreed. Starting off with a 761 series, she whipped the men by more than 100 pins combined and walked off with the cash.

Whether it was for money or pride, Warmbier was determined to roll her best. However, once, in 1934, as a favor, Warmbier bowled with the young niece of a friend. In an attempt not to show up the teenager, Warmbier tied the girl 196–196. The friend then needled Warmbier, saying that the bowler perhaps wasn't as great as everyone thought.

Flashing eyes of fire, Warmbier sat her friend and the girl down in the settee, grabbed a ball, and said, "Now watch closely."

Warmbier promptly rattled off twelve straight strikes. Turning to the aunt and niece, she added, "Let's make this a baker's dozen." Then she threw her thirteenth consecutive strike.

The Long (John) and Short of It

John Kuth hated foul judges as much as he did 10-pin taps.

In the days before automatic foul detectors, foul judges were a fixture at every bowling tournament. The judge would sit on a high-legged stool alongside one end of the lanes and bang a gong, blow a whistle, press a buzzer, or just shout whenever an errant bowler slipped past the foul line.

During the 1934 ABC Tournament in Peoria, Illinois, Kuth, a bowler from Milwaukee, had been buzzed twice by the foul judge. Both times, Kuth uttered an epithet or two and continued bowling.

In the middle of his final game of the day, Kuth nailed his fourth straight strike when he again was singled out by the foul judge for crossing the foul line. This time, the bowler boiled over with fury, stormed over to the foul judge, and began berating him unmercifully.

At the height of his tirade, Kuth flailed his arms with such wild intensity that the trouser buttons which were attached to his suspenders broke off. His pants dropped faster than a head pin and wound up in a heap around his ankles.

Kuth's temper tantrum came to an abrupt halt as he stood speechless in his long johns. For a split second, the bowling alley turned deadly quiet. Then the place erupted in raucous laughter. Kuth's face, which had been red from anger, remained red—only this time from embarrassment.

He didn't utter another peep to the foul judge throughout the rest of the tournament.

Blowin' Smoke

ABC Hall of Famer Walter "The Cigar" Ward earned his nickname by always bowling with a short, black stogie tightly clenched in the right side of his mouth.

To the All-Star bowler of the 1930s, 1940s, and early 1950s, a cigar was as much a part of his equipment as his bowling ball. The way he treated his cigar told much about how he was bowling.

If his ball began to hook too severely or if he couldn't find the pocket, Ward would yank the stogie out of his mouth and throw it against the wall. Sometimes he would slam it to the floor and stomp on it. One time, when his opponent struck out in the final frame to beat him, Ward stuffed his cigar into the bowler's drink. Of course, if Ward won, he would puff contentedly on a new stogie.

"One time during a tournament I had just tossed away a pretty good cigar with most of it going into the cuspidor," Ward recalled. "Someone from the audience offered me a new one and I was hesitant, fearing a practical joke.

"But I lighted it and it proved all right while I was bowling. However, I wasn't doing well because I kept getting those darn 10-pin taps. With disgust, I threw away the cigar. There was no cuspidor handy, so I just flung it at the wall. Imagine my surprise when it exploded like a bomb! I'll always be thankful for those taps."

Bowling's Bad Boy

Of all the bowlers on the pro circuit, PBA Hall of Famer Marshall Holman is the one people love to hate.

He's the McEnroe of the lanes—raging at his own screwups as well as his opponents' good fortune. When Holman blows a strike, he often stomps his feet, punches the ball return, or kicks the settee. When an opponent makes a big shot, Holman sometimes sticks his fingers in his ears to drown out the cheers of the crowd.

"He's not so much poetry in motion as he is mayhem in motion," noted bowling columnist Jim Dressel.

Entering 1994 with twenty-one titles under his belt, Holman is the PBA's all-time leading money winner with $1,606,961 in earnings. But the top winner has been known to be a sore loser.

Once, during a match, opponent Jeff Mattingly needed to get three strikes in the tenth frame to beat Holman. When Mattingly got his first strike, Holman kicked a chair and sent it rattling against the approach. When Mattingly nailed his second strike, Holman kicked the ball rack.

When Mattingly tossed the third strike, Holman threw a fit—and nearly everything else in sight.

During the 1980s, bowling's bad boy was racking up as many conduct violations as he was four-baggers.

His costliest outburst erupted in front of a nationwide TV audience during the 1980 Showboat Doubles Classic. Tommy Hudson and Pete Couture were pitted against Holman and Mark Roth in the finals. The lead seesawed back and forth and came down to the tenth frame. Couture, needing a strike, left a solid 10-pin on his first toss. Now all Holman needed was a strike to lock up his team's third crown in four years. But he left the bucket.

Holman was so furious that he kicked the foul light unit with all his might and broke it. Metal pieces flew through the air as the smashed unit buzzed out of control.

Couture then calmly spared, clinching a narrow 466–464 victory and $20,000 for his team while runners-up Holman and Roth split $12,000.

Because Holman was already under probation for prior misbehavior, the PBA suspended him for ten tournaments and fined him $2,500 for his impromptu punt.

The punishment didn't do much good in curbing his temper. Two years later at the Firestone Tournament of Champions, Holman blew up after leaving the 10-pin. The infuriated bowler walked to the back of the settee and slammed his fist into a retaining wall in a fit of frustration. Unfortunately, his tantrum left him with a broken right hand.

"Can you believe it?" Holman once said in *Bowlers*

Journal. "People have come up to me and told me they think I'm disgusting, that they'd rather watch someone just go up and throw the ball and then sit down. Sure. And they like to watch the test pattern on their TV set, too.

"A woman once wrote that she turns off the set when I'm on the telecast. Frankly, I didn't believe her because why take the trouble to write and insult me if you don't watch?

"Bowling fans would be upset if I were to make a drastic change. I think they enjoy watching me get excited, and getting angry at the pins. If they didn't have anyone to root against, it wouldn't be any fun."

Pranks for the Memories

Throughout his remarkable career, Joe Norris was known for his devilish pranks almost as much as he was for his skills as a Hall of Fame bowler.

He never missed an opportunity to pull a practical joke.

Norris once taped a huge chunk of smelly Limburger cheese to the underside of a desk occupied by a dour ABC official who grew increasingly irritable as the sickening odor from the decaying cheese turned even riper.

Andy Glavas, a masseur in the paddock at many ABC tournaments in the 1940s, became a favorite Norris target. During one All-Star tourney, the bowlers were grumbling about a rank odor coming from Glavas. His massage business quickly fizzled.

"How come you boys don't come back for a rubdown anymore?" he asked one of the bowlers.

"Frankly, Andy, you ought to take a shower," the bowler replied.

Glavas, who assumed the smell came from the bowlers, said, "I was just going to tell you guys the same thing."

Glavas decided something fishy was going on. He was right—literally. The masseur discovered that the mischievous Norris had nailed a dead fish to the bottom of the massage table.

During a 1952 tournament in Milwaukee, Norris spotted *Bowling Journal* publisher Mort Luby, Sr., getting ticketed for jaywalking. So the bowler decided to make life even more miserable for Luby.

"He's a big troublemaker, Officer," Norris told the policeman. "You ought to check out his record. His mug shot is on the walls of every post office in the country."

The gullible cop hauled a protesting Luby off to the police station. Figuring Luby had experienced enough fun, Norris went down to spring his pal. The prankster confessed to the cops that it was all a joke, but they didn't believe him at first. They kept a now furious Luby behind bars for several hours before learning that he had a clean record—although he threatened, upon his release, to murder Norris.

When Carmen Salvino joined Norris's Tri Par Radio team in 1954, Norris invited him over to the house—and welcomed him with a stomach-churning practical joke. "I told him I was thirsty and he told me to go to the refrigerator and help myself," Salvino recalled. "I opened the door and there were six green 7-Up bottles. I took one, opened it, and started gulping. I must have had the thing half empty before I discovered I was drinking white vinegar, not 7-Up! The first thing I grabbed for was my throat, and the second was Norris's throat." Salvino later learned that Norris had filled all six bottles with vinegar.

No one was safe from Norris's pranks—not even his wife Billie. "I gave up dusting Joe's trophy room," she once said. "He had the place booby-trapped. Every time I'd move something, there'd be an explosion."

If he wasn't passing out exploding cigars, Norris was cutting people's ties in half. But every once in a while, someone would try to get even.

One day, Norris showed up at ABC headquarters with brightly painted Easter eggs. He doled out the eggs to his friends and began explaining what he called an old Lithuanian custom. "You just put one of these Easter eggs on your head and tap on it lightly," he told them.

ABC field representative Charlie Fleming suspected a trap. So he sneaked up behind Norris, who was demonstrating this "custom," and slapped him on top of the head. The shell shattered and raw egg slithered down Norris's head.

But Norris got the last laugh. When Fleming went to get his bowling ball a few days later, he discovered that someone had drilled an enormous hole in it, filled it with dirt, and planted a daisy.

Having a Little Fling

One of the classic bowling pranks of all time was pulled off in 1933.

Milo Wiesner, who owned a bowling alley in Chicago, and friends Leo Rollick and Johnny Wallen were part of a team who traveled to nearby Aurora, Illinois, to compete in a tournament. Unfortunately, the trio bowled terribly.

Lugging their bowling bags, the men left the alley and began walking across a bridge over the Fox River when Wiesner was struck with a devilish thought. He suggested that the three of them fling their equipment over the railing and into the river. Still stinging from getting badly whipped on the lanes, Rollick and Wallen agreed.

"Okay," said Wiesner, "on the count of three." While Wallen was peering over the railing, Wiesner winked to Rollick, who winked back. Swinging their bowling bags to build up momentum, the trio shouted in unison, "One, two, three!"

Wallen let go of his bowling bag, launching it on a journey to oblivion. A split-second later, he got a sickening sensation when he realized that his two pals had held onto their bags. All he could do was watch his bag with his favorite ball inside sail over the side of the bridge and into the murky water below.

"I've been had!" he bellowed in dismay. Rather than explode in rage, he joined in the laughter.

"Tell you what," said Wiesner. "On league nights, I'll let you use any ball from my alley for nothing."

Over the next few weeks, Wallen tried different balls from Wiesner's alley, but none of them felt right. One night, Wiesner gave Wallen a ball that he said belonged to a friend. With it, Wallen bowled his best series since the prank—an impressive 685.

"I've got to buy this ball," Wallen told him.

"The owner can't sell it to you," said Wiesner.

"Tell me who owns it," said Wallen. "I'll make him a good proposition."

"Well," said Wiesner with a big grin, "if you had looked at the ball closely, you would have known that it was your own—the same one you tossed into the Fox River!"

Wiesner then revealed that co-conspirator Leo Rollick had felt so guilty about Wallen's lost ball that he fished it out of the river the day after the prank. Rollick planned to give it back to Wallen right away, but Wiesner wanted to wait so he could pull off one more practical joke on Wallen.

Buffaloed Bowlers

For a reason that defies explanation, the bowling balls of competitors in the Buffalo Classic were favorite targets of pranksters.

In 1946, W.W. Edgar of Detroit shuffled off to Buffalo with the happy anticipation of bowling in a big tournament. On the evening of his first match, Edgar went to his assigned lane and reached into his bag, but had trouble trying to pull out his ball. Edgar couldn't find the finger holes. That's because there weren't any. A prankster back in Detroit had swiped Edgar's ball and replaced it with one that had no holes. The irked bowler was forced to get a hasty drill job on his new ball.

In the same tournament, Red Irwin, former president of the ABC, was victimized by a hometown buddy. When Irwin got off the train in Buffalo, he told a companion that his bowling bag felt unusually heavy. Irwin opened his bag, and to his shock, discovered that his ball had been replaced by a twenty-pound lead weight. Irwin made a frantic call to his wife, who promptly air-mailed his ball to him, which arrived just in the nick of time before his first match. "Gosh," Irwin recalled, "the mailing expense was more than the price of another ball."

Twenty-five years earlier, Walter Schuster of Chicago unknowingly traveled to the 1921 tournament with a cement ball in his bag. Not until he arrived in Buffalo did he realize that he had been victimized by a prankster.

Roll Models

Unusual Balls

Soaking It All In

In 1973, pro bowlers were making a bizarre bet: Which bowler would be the first to accidentally blow up his motel room?

That's because the pros became caught up in the short-lived craze of soaking their bowling balls in a dangerously volatile solvent. It was their radical "solution" to changes in lane conditions.

By 1970, bowling centers began using a new, harder finish to cover the lanes on the pro tour. It was much less flammable and much more durable than the old finish, saving money in maintenance and insurance. Meanwhile, bowling balls were being made of harder plastic materials. As a result, hard balls on the hard lanes caused what should have been good shots to skid. Because the ball wasn't grabbing as it once did, bowlers were having trouble throwing hooks.

In 1973, pro bowler Don McCune went looking for a solution that would soften his bowling ball so it would better grab the lane. After getting a list of solvents from a chemist, McCune poured one called toluene into a five-gallon can and dropped his ball in it overnight. The next morning, he was able to indent the ball's surface with a thumbnail. Prior to using the solvent, he couldn't even scratch the ball with a knife.

McCune promptly took the ball to a local bowling center near his home in Munster, Indiana. A bowling lane is thirty-nine boards wide, and until that day, McCune's ball had been hooking over only three or four boards. On this day, it was hooking ten or more. He wound up rolling a nifty 763 series.

McCune had won only two PBA tournaments in the previous ten years as a pro. But early in 1973, he won back-to-back titles with his soaked ball. "Everyone was going crazy," he recalled. "They suspected something, so I told them I was using a soft-surface ball. But that's all."

Before long, as McCune continued to win or place high in tourney after tourney, word spread among the bowlers that he was soaking his ball. So they began using "soakers," the name given balls softened by leaving them overnight in a solution known as MEK—methyl ethyl ketone. But MEK was also toxic and highly flammable. Breathing it could cause brain damage and destroy the lungs. As one cautious pro told *Sports Illustrated* back then, "I'd rather carry a hand grenade in my pocket than use that stuff."

Two weeks after McCune won his second back-to-back titles of the year, twenty-two of the twenty-four finalists at the 1973 Houston-Sertoma Open were using soakers. The qualifying average was 214, eight points higher than the previous year.

Bill Taylor, an expert on bowling balls, became alarmed over the increasing number of pros who were rolling soakers. Warned Taylor, "At this rate [of growing popularity], it won't be long before an Eskimo living outside Fairbanks, Alaska, will blast his wife, his igloo, and his bowling ball into the Bering Sea."

Fortunately, no bowler accidentally blew up his home or his hotel room. However, soaking did trigger at least one wild and crazy mishap.

One night, later that same year, fourteen bowlers were staying in the same motel during a PBA tournament in Illinois. When guests complained of a pungent odor, the motel owner discovered that all the bowlers were soaking balls in buckets of the dangerous solvent in their rooms.

"Get those damn balls out of my motel!" he ordered. "The whole place could explode!"

The bowlers complied and lugged their pails full of solvent and balls and grouped the buckets together outside in an empty parking space in the lot. Later, in the wee hours of the morning, a weary motorist pulled into the motel. He pulled into what he thought was an empty parking space—and crashed his car smack dab into the pails, knocking them over.

Banging, bouncing bowling balls scattered over the lot, which, as luck would have it, was situated on a hill. The balls plowed into cars, bushes, and each other as they bounded their way out of the lot and down the street.

With all the commotion, lights in motel rooms were flicked on by startled motel guests who hurried to their windows. From their vantage point, the guests watched more than a dozen pro bowlers in various stages of undress scrambling through the night trying to recover their precious bowling balls, including a few which ended up more than a block away.

By the end of the year, most pros realized it wasn't worth dealing with highly dangerous and unstable chemicals—especially since some solvents had been banned because of their highly explosive nature. Besides, companies had begun making pre-softened bowling balls which made soakers obsolete.

Meanwhile, McCune enjoyed the best season of his career in 1973, earning $69,000. He had become the year's biggest money winner, finishing first in six tourneys. However, when the soaking craze ended, so did McCune's money-winning days.

Dodo Balls

After the ABC set the rules and standardized the equipment in 1895, bowlers still found ways to doctor their ball so it would roll in a certain predictable way.

They did this by making a dodo ball—one that was illegally weighted.

At the turn of the century, several craftsmen set up a side business in creating the dodo ball. By putting extra weight on the ball's hitting side (the left for a right-handed bowler), the ball would hook to the left. The result was more power delivered to the pin on impact.

Oscar Holberg, one of the top bowlers of that era, was said to roll a ball so heavily loaded that, as one sports writer put it, "it would walk in and pick off the 5–7–10 without any great difficulty."

Before the ABC outlawed dodo balls in sanctioned play in 1913, Steve Geroux, a well-known bowler and craftsmen, earned a reputation for making the finest dodo balls around. Geroux would delicately slice a fourteen-pound wooden ball and an eighteen-pound ball in half. Then, using dowels and glue, he would join the two halves together. He smoothed out the joint on a lathe so that no one could tell the ball was doctored.

Only once did Geroux's talents betray him. One of his dodo balls had been banged up pretty badly from too much use. But he still chose to play with it. However, while trying to pick up a 7–10 split during a league game, Geroux lofted the ball too much. It crashed on the alley and split in two. Incredibly, according to witnesses who swear it happened, one half of the ball toppled the 7-pin while the other half took out the 10.

Geroux claimed he should be credited with converting the split. His opponents vehemently disagreed, so a judge was called for a ruling.

"Sorry, Steve," said the judge. "But the only split you've made is the one with your ball, not the pins. Mark down an 8."

Sexy Rhonda Shear, TV hostess of USA Network's "Up All Night," modeled nude for a Playboy *magazine photo shoot at a bowling center in Milwaukee in 1993. The center kept several lanes open for bowlers to use while Rhonda posed for the photography crew. It was then that Rhonda learned the bare truth about bowlers. "Here I was naked, doing splits in a bowling alley, and ten lanes away, guys weren't even looking," Rhonda lamented. "I mean, those were serious bowlers!"*

Sinking Into Obscurity

At the turn of the century, the Brunswick-Balk-Collender Co. introduced the Tifco ball, claiming it was the wave of the future.

Instead, the ball quickly sank from sight.

In marked contrast to the wooden balls still in vogue at the time, the Tifco was brightly colored and made of rubber with a rubber core.

But Tifcos weren't all that reliable. They tended to swell as they warmed up from use on the lanes. With each game bowled, the ball would grow several fractions of an inch, to the point that they would enlarge to beyond the legal limit of 27 inches in circumference. So owners of Tifcos found a strange solution. They would keep the balls in the ice box until the day before they were scheduled to bowl!

In 1910, a large group of bowlers from Toledo, Ohio, purchased new Tifco balls for the ABC's annual tournament in Detroit. Unfortunately for the Toledo bowlers, they all bowled badly in the tourney. The highest score that year with a Tifco was a lowly 539 for a three-game series.

The chagrined Toledo bowlers returned home and decided to make a joint statement about their feelings toward their Tifcos. The bowlers met in the middle of a bridge over the Maumee River. On the count of three, they all hurled their bowling balls into the water.

Recalled one of the ball-tossers, "I can still hear that 'ker-plunk' as each ball hit the water. If those balls had only floated, they would surely have made some sight. But we never wanted to see them again."

Like the ones tossed into the river, Tifcos soon sank in popularity.

The Old Ball Game

No bowling ball had been rolled so often for so long as the one bought by Charlie Schrull.

The ball was used continuously for an amazing sixty-three years!

Back at the turn of the century, most bowlers used wooden balls that had a tendency to change shape with the rise or fall of the temperature and humidity. The wooden balls also had the nasty habit of chipping around the finger holes.

When hard rubber balls were introduced in 1905, Schrull, a New Yorker, was one of the first keglers to purchase one for the lofty price (by yesterday's standards) of $20. He bought it because the ball was guaranteed to hold its shape for three years.

It held up a lot longer than that.

From then on, it was the only ball Schrull ever used during league competition. When he died, he willed the ball to his son George, who used it two times a week in regular league play.

Finally, in 1968, George, of Bronxville, New York, decided the ball had outlived its usefulness on the lanes. With some sadness, he retired the ball, which today sits in a collection of famous balls at the National Bowling Hall of Fame and Museum.

The Deep Six

Police in Troy, New York, rushed into action one day in 1985 after receiving a report from witnesses that a suspicious man had thrown something off the Troy-Menands Bridge into the dark waters of the Hudson River.

Siren-screaming squad cars sped to the scene, but the police found nothing. With the help of a tugboat, the authorities dredged the river under the bridge and came up with a neatly tied heavy package. They opened it cautiously and found . . . a bowling ball!

It was traced to William Biette, thirty-six, of Wynantskill. He told police he had a real bad night during his league play and had given the ball the deep six because "it let me down."

* * *

In 1981, during the annual ABC convention, members of the Bowling Writers Association enjoyed a luncheon aboard the Mississippi River paddlewheel *Delta Queen*. They began kidding Long Island bowling columnist Bob Zellner about his dismal showing in the writers' own bowling tournament.

"Bob, since we're on the Mississippi, I'll give you a buck if you throw your ball into the river," one of the scribes said. Zellner accepted the offer and, amid much picture-taking and joking, tossed his sixteen-pound ball into the mighty Mississippi.

No sooner had the ball sank below the muddy waters then Zellner realized he had made a terrible mistake. He turned to his fellow writers and said, "Now, I'll give $50 to the one who returns it to me."

No one took him up on the offer.

Hot Shot

Dick Berger learned that having a hot ball doesn't necessarily mean it's mowing down strike after strike.

At a 1968 session of the Los Angeles Traveling League at the Arcadia Bowl, Berger and teammate Gary Yamauchi were tossing warm-up throws when the pinsetting machine malfunctioned. Both balls became trapped in the machine when a pin jammed. The belt rubbing against the pin created so much friction that it caught fire and the balls of Yamauchi and Berger were scorched before the fire was put out.

Because there wasn't enough time to get new equipment, both bowlers decided to use their hot bowling balls. Unfortunately, Yamauchi played cold all night and wound up with only a 575 series.

But Berger enjoyed a hot ball, both figuratively and literally. With his scorched ball, he rolled a 689 series—the highest for the league that night and the best Berger had scored the entire season.

"Maybe I should burn my ball every week," he joked.

In 1984, ABC Hall of Famer Ed Lubanski went to Niagara Falls to bowl in his thirty-third ABC tournament. But he had to withdraw—because his bowling ball rolled off the motel bed and broke his toe!

Tour De Farce

In 1915, a bowling ball embarked on an ambitious tour of the world that took eighteen years to complete.

During the trip, it was accused of being a bomb and a spy; was jettisoned overboard on a sinking ship; was saved and then lost but found again; and finally was returned to the United States where it received star treatment.

To advertise its latest model, the Brunswick-Balk-Collender Co. decided to send a new Mineralite ball—No. 391914—on a tour of YMCAs around the globe. Company officials proudly demonstrated the ball at the 1915 Panama Pacific Exposition in San Francisco and then carefully packed it in a wooden box and sent it on a worldwide journey that proved to be a wild ride.

The ball traveled by train to New York where it was placed on the S.S. *Mauritania* for a transatlantic voyage to the United Kingdom. The ball was given VIP treatment as bowlers tried it out at YMCA bowling alleys in Liverpool, England; Belfast, Ireland; Glasgow, Scotland; and London.

Then the Mineralite crossed the English channel to Denmark. From there, it was slated to go to Berlin, Germany, for use in an exhibition. However, World War I interfered with its travel plans and it was lost.

A report to Brunswick from an agent for Wells Fargo—the company entrusted with the ball's safety throughout its journey—stated: "The last advice we had of the ball was that it was en route to Berlin. Taking into consideration the appearance of the ball (somewhat like a bomb) and conditions abroad, I will be surprised if we ever see or hear anything of the shipment again. There is at present no opportunity of getting any information concerning it."

The ball never made it to Germany. For weeks no one knew of the Mineralite's whereabouts.

Back in the United States, newspaper accounts claimed the ball had fallen into enemy hands. One story declared the ball had been "arrested as a spy" while another stated it was confiscated "as a cannon ball in disguise" and "as a contraband of war." In the most outrageous report, a New York paper claimed the ball had been "seized as ammunition by the Germans and used in one of the big Krupp guns to turn the tide of battle by mowing down a regiment or two of the enemy."

None of the stories were true. Instead, the ball somehow ended up in France where shipping agents there cabled Brunswick, "We have duly received the bowling ball No. 391914, but under present conditions the intended trip of the ball is compromised. We shall, therefore, keep it in Paris, pending your instructions."

Brunswick ordered the ball returned to England, where shipping agents arranged for it to bypass the war. The ball was sent by ship to Bombay, India, for an exhibition. Then it was placed aboard the vessel *Nubia*, which was bound for Sydney, Australia.

But once again, the ball was lost. One report stated that the *Nubia* had been requisitioned as part of the war effort and all cargo was unloaded in Ceylon (now called Sri Lanka). Much to the dismay of Brunswick, no one knew the fate of the cargo.

However, weeks later, the company received another message. The good news was that the ship had not been requisitioned after all. The bad news was, well, bad. According to William Gillanders, secretary of the YMCA in Sydney, Australia, "Advices from Bombay Forwarding Firm state that the P.&O. liner *Nubia* has gone ashore on a coral reef off Mativell. Ship in bad way. Cargo being jettisoned last report and with fine weather it is hoped vessel might be floated. Looks as if ball had met watery grave."

It certainly appeared that way. Brunswick officials remained optimistic only because, in the past, whenever the ball seemed lost, it would eventually show up. But weeks turned into months and months turned into years without a single word about the fate of the ball.

Then, incredibly, in 1932, someone at the Wells Fargo Company in Sydney stumbled across the ball in its shipping crate in a warehouse. How it got there no one knows. But the people at Brunswick were ecstatic.

The ball was placed aboard the S.S. *Maitai* and delivered with fanfare to its starting place in San Francisco in early 1933. The Mineralite had completed a harrowing eighteen-year journey around the world. But its travel days weren't over. The ball was sent—without further mishap—to the Century of Progress in Chicago, where thousands marveled at it for all it had gone through.

So where is the ball today? No one knows. Somehow, it was lost again and the people at Brunswick don't know where it is. However, they did find the shipping crate in which the ball traveled. The box is now safe and sound at the National Bowling Hall of Fame and Museum.

Masquerade Balls

Not content to roll a sixteen-pound ball that's twenty-seven inches in circumference down a sixty-foot lane to topple ten three-and-a-half-pound wooden pins, bowlers have reached new heights—or depths, depending on your point of view—in creating new variations of their favorite sport. For example:

Biosphere Bowling—Popularized in 1992 at a Manhattan bar called Aces and 8's, bowlers not only have a ball, they are *in* the ball. Two-person teams compete against each other for free drinks. The bowlee of each team crawls into a sphere four feet in diameter made of one-inch steel tubes, clings to hand grips, and is strapped into a seat. Then his partner shoves the sphere in a wild, end-over-end, thirty-foot ride to a set of six five-foot-tall canvas pins stuffed with foam.

One of the drawbacks in this game is that the bowlee might hurl his lunch while hurtling down the alley.

Inventor Thomas Bell came up with the idea of Biosphere Bowling after watching a gerbil running inside its wheel. Said Bell, "It's the greatest thing to happen to bowling since Chris Schenkel."

* * *

Body Bowling—Who needs a ball? Just toss your friend down the length of the bar. Created by the Taurus Steakhouse in Coconut Grove, Florida, in 1989, the game began when several patrons were bragging about their bowling styles. One thing led to another and when one man offered his services as a human bowling ball, the craze was born. His buddies tossed him across the floor where he knocked over ten empty beer bottles.

Since its humble beginnings, body bowling has been fine-tuned. A slippery mat is used for an alley and the pins are inflatable plastic bottles. The bowler grabs his human bowlee and flings him down the makeshift lane and into the pins. It has become more exhibition than competition because onlookers rate the performance on style and originality of both the bowler and bowlee.

What significance does body bowling hold for Americans? Late-night TV talk show host David Letterman has the answer. The sport, he told his audience, signals "the end of society as we know it."

* * *

Turkey Bowling—Derrick Johnson dreamed up the sport in 1988 while working as a night stocker in a Newport Beach, California, supermarket. As a joke, his store manager slid a frozen turkey toward him and it knocked over a soda bottle. "Boom! The basic idea for the sport was born," Johnson recalled.

Johnson established rules, including terms such as "gobbler" (three straight strikes) and "wishbone" (a 7–10 split). The founder of turkey bowling slides a frozen Butterball turkey down a supermarket aisle to knock down ten full two-liter plastic soda pop bottles set up like bowling pins forty-five feet from the "fowl" line.

He has raised thousands of dollars for charity by enlisting sponsors for turkey bowling.

But some corporations have done their best to knock the stuffing out of the sport. In 1989, the Swift-Eckrich company wrote Johnson a letter threatening to sue him if he didn't stop bowling with Butterballs. It claimed he was damaging the "quality image" of their product.

"Their threatening letter is really fowl play," said Johnson. "I use Butterballs because they're simply the best on the market. They're frozen so hard they are practically indestructible. Some people take themselves too seriously. Pepsi paid me $3,000 *not* to use their bottle. Come on, guys, loosen up."

Johnson appointed himself commissioner of the PBA—the Poultry Bowling Association—which now claims 2,500 members.

"I have to admit, this thing has mushroomed into total stupidity," he said. "I guess it's because this is a sport that's poultry in motion."

Loony Lanes

Weird Alleys

Bowling (Off) Center

So who says a bowling lane has to be inside a bowling center?

Bowlers have enjoyed the game in a wide range of venues from a jetliner to a major league ballpark. For instance:

In 1962, Hall of Famers Sylvia Wene and Dick Weber reached new heights in bowling—about 30,000 feet high. In what was billed as "Operation Astro-Bowl," a bowling lane was set up inside an American Airlines Boeing 707 cargo plane, complete with an automatic pinsetter.

As a publicity stunt, AMF arranged for Weber to play Wene on a flight from New York to Dallas. While flying at a speed of nearly 600 mph, Wene defeated Weber 144–141. Later, Weber, with tongue in cheek, accused the pilots of altering the course of his ball by changing altitude and making turns a second after his releases.

* * *

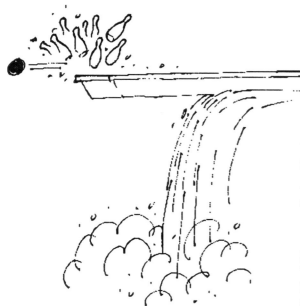

In 1985, Sheridan Lanes of Niagara Falls, New York, built a forty-five-foot lane, complete with gutters, ball rack, and tenpins—on a raft! As a benefit for the American Cancer Society, people paid to bowl on the raft as it floated down the Niagara River.

* * *

During World War II, workers at the Boeing airplane factory discovered that the C-97 transport plane was long enough to house a bowling lane. Employees liked to bowl inside the seventy-eight foot fuselage because it had no gutters.

* * *

When he was president, Harry Truman had four bowling lanes built in the basement of the White House. Although he may have enjoyed the game, he wasn't very good at it. Maybe it was because he often bowled in his wing-tip shoes.

The lanes remained in the basement into Richard Nixon's administration. Nixon, the most avid bowler of all the presidents, reluctantly agreed to have the lanes moved to the Executive Office Building because the basement space was needed for his national security advisers.

* * *

Andy Varipapa, one of the world's greatest trick-shot artists, once bowled at Crosley Field, then home of the Cincinnati Reds. In 1955, a specially installed lane, complete with ball return, was built along the third base line from the bag to home plate. In front of a cheering crowd before the baseball game, Varipapa put on a dazzling bowling exhibition.

* * *

The first bowling center in California was a giant redwood tree!

In 1866, bored loggers chopped down a monster tree. It fell with such force that it was embedded in the ground. The loggers then cut the tree in half lengthwise and, by careful leveling and planing, carved out a bowling alley. In fact, the tree was so wide that they were able to make two lanes side by side. Using some of the wood from the other half of the tree, the loggers constructed a wood shed over the lanes and added ball returns and backstops.

In the 1950s, Lucky Strike cigarettes offered to sponsor a bowling team captained by ABC Hall of Famer Buddy Bomar. But Bomar refused, explaining, "Who wants to be associated with lucky strikes? When we get 'em, we want to earn 'em."

It's All There In Black and White

Leave it to television executives to come up with a gimmicky idea.

Convinced that viewers of "The Major League Bowling Show" had a hard time seeing the ball, the TV execs decided that changes had to be made on the program. So they ordered the lanes painted black and the balls painted white.

On May 23, 1959, at the Neptune Lanes in Brooklyn, the match was televised with the white balls on the black lanes.

Not surprisingly, the new look delivered the impact of a gutter ball. Viewer response was so negative it was never tried again.

Feelin' Groovy

The year 1965 was the "grooviest" in bowling history.

That was when dozens of bowling centers in Omaha, Detroit, and Milwaukee were caught doctoring their lanes for the benefit of the bowlers.

Until that year, the 32,000 league bowlers in Omaha averaged about fifty series with scores of over 700 during a typical winter season. But then, all at once, more than two hundred such series were rolled.

While bowlers and proprietors were thrilled, the ABC was suspicious. An investigation revealed that after the last bowler had gone home for the night, many bowling center operators were busy sanding, roughing, oiling, and polishing their lanes. These ingenious tricks were designed to make it easier for bowlers to roll high scores so that even a little old lady could ring up a 700 series.

Most proprietors relied on a secret way to create a ball track that imperceptibly guided the ball into the pocket. A strip of oil about twenty inches wide was left on each lane by the automatic lane conditioning machines. That way, the ball hugged the oil and rolled into the pocket.

After the investigation spread to other parts of the country, the ABC threw out ninety of the 108 top scores; eighteen perfect games; the nation's highest team score, which was rolled in Detroit; and dozens of 700 series in Milwaukee.

Nevertheless, lane fixing continued to plague the game. In 1968, all twenty-six bowling centers in Portland, Oregon, received official warnings that continued doctoring of lanes would result in cancellation of their ABC certification.

But that didn't stop a scandal from brewing in Des Moines, Iowa, months later. The averages of the 16,000 league bowlers in the city jumped by almost 10 points per person. Games of 200 or more were coming faster than league secretaries could record them. But then the ABC sleuths moved in, lanes were resurfaced, and scores returned to normal.

"All bowlers want to roll better scores," explained Paul Harvey, of Des Moines, owner of the Earl Best Bowling Center, who asked for the ABC probe. "So when they find that at certain lanes their scores zoom up, that's where they want to roll. Meanwhile, those of us who follow the regulations start losing business. Pretty soon, in self-defense, almost everybody is tampering with the lanes."

When the *Des Moines Register and Tribune* exposed the scandal, the paper was flooded with letters from outraged bowlers—and from keglers who didn't see anything wrong with the doctored alleys. Wrote one bowler: "What's so bad about making the lanes better for scoring? Don't the sporting goods people put out golf balls that we can belt further, and make us look like better golfers? Well, why shouldn't bowlers get a break?"

Is There a Doctor in the House?

During the 1940s, bowling teams would do anything to get the edge on the competition—especially by doctoring the lanes.

Once, in 1948, Buddy Bomar, who was later inducted into the ABC Hall of Fame, captained the Tavern Pale team when it met the E&B club from Detroit for the national championship. In those days, major titles were often decided in a home-and-home competition. The teams would bowl a series at each other's home lanes with total pins deciding the winner.

The E&Bs took the lead after the first series in Detroit. But Bomar had a cunning trick up his sleeve to all but guarantee that he and his boys would win the title.

Bomar's home base was Samuelson's Bowl in Chicago, which, like most other centers at the time, coated its lanes with shellac. Bomar knew that shellac turned very hard when the temperature dropped. Since it was winter, he opened the windows in the bowling center several days before the match so the shellac felt like ice. Then he buffed the lanes to make them even slicker.

Connie McColley, of Baldin, South Carolina, gave a good first impression, but unfortunately it didn't last. In the first game of her debut on the Ladies Pro Bowlers Tour in 1986, she rolled a perfect game. But she failed to reach 200 in her next seventeen games, and finished the tournament dead last.

Bomar had his team practice in sweaters and scarves while they learned to handle the slippery lane conditions in the freezing bowling center. On match day, he didn't turn the heat up at Samuelson's until the last minute. By then, it was much too late for the shellac to "thaw" on the lanes.

Unable to handle the slick alleys, the E&Bs easily were downed by the Tavern Pale team. From then on, Bomar was given a new nickname by his fellow bowlers—"Buffy."

* * *

Buzz Fazio, another ABC Hall of Famer, had some of Bomar's larceny in him.

In the days of the short-lived National Bowling League, Carmen Salvino's Dallas team went to Omaha to bowl Fazio's squad. "Buzz had a bunch of straight ball bowlers, so he laid strips of masking tape from the right sides of the foul lines to the pockets and then had the lanes oiled heavily," Salvino recalled. "His boys could use that dry strip like a track, while the hookers on my team were sliding all over the place. It wasn't against the rules, so all we could do was complain." And lose.

Freeze Frame

Talk about slick lanes and cold shooting. The 1904 ABC National Championship Tournament in Cleveland had plenty of both—literally.

The arena which held the tourney was so frigid inside that ice formed on the lanes and competitors were forced to bowl in heavy winter gear.

Held in the middle of winter when the temperatures barely hovered above zero, the tournament took place in a drafty, leaky, freezing armory. The building was heated by only six old furnaces that proved totally inadequate in warming up the place. In fact, it was so cold inside that when the bowlers spit, it would freeze in the cuspidors.

Bowlers were forced to don heavy winter garb during their matches. Many wore ear muffs, mittens, and overcoats between shots. Others drank up to four ounces of whiskey a game in a futile effort to keep warm.

"Competitors could be seen shivering as they delivered the ball," said one newspaper account. "They might as well have been bowling outside in the winter air for all the good the furnaces did."

Adding to their woes, a leaky roof allowed melted snow to drip onto the lanes, where it promptly froze, halting play numerous times until the ice was cleared off.

Because of the ridiculously harsh conditions, scores were at their lowest ever for the tournament. The cold also kept the spectators away. "There were not enough people at the games to form a cinch [card] party," reported the *Chicago Tribune*. "The promoters suffered a financial loss of by no means small proportions—and were given no sympathy by anyone who was in attendance."

The Perfect Ending

Amazing 300 Games

Mr. 900

Before he threw his first ball in the Thursday night bowling league, Glenn Allison told his girlfriend Jessie Thompson that he'd roll a 300 game for her birthday.

Allison did better than that. He achieved bowling immortality by rolling a flawless string of three consecutive 300 games for a perfect 900 series.

It all began on July 1, 1982, when Allison, fifty-two, who spent thirteen years on the pro bowling circuit, arrived at the La Habra 300 Bowl near his hometown of Whittier, California. He was set to take part in a three-person mixed league match in which Jessie was the anchor girl on the opposing team.

"Because it's your birthday, I'm going to roll you a perfect game," he promised her. Then Allison fired a strike on his first ball.

A half hour later, he kept his word by tossing his twelfth straight strike. "See, I never break my promise," he beamed to Jessie.

When his sister-in-law Wilma Allison complained that she was in the bowling center's restaurant and had missed seeing his perfect game, Allison told her, "Well, there's always the chance I'll throw another." Thirty minutes later, Allison skillfully launched his twenty-fourth consecutive strike for back-to-back 300s. He gave a little arm pump as the pins in the final frame crashed and then he proudly walked back to the growing cluster of amazed onlookers.

The bowling center buzzed with excitement. Could he do the impossible—roll a perfect series? For the next half hour, whenever Allison stepped onto the approach to Lane 13 or 14, the place fell eerily silent. Bowlers on the other thirty lanes waited respectfully. Waitresses tiptoed by with their trays of beer. But once Allison's ball was safely on its way, shouts and exhortations broke the quiet. With each crash of the pins, cheers and applause filled the air.

At the end of the eighth frame, Allison wormed through the throng of spectators and gulped down two shots of whiskey. "I'm nervous," he whispered to his brother Bob. "My knees are shaking." Allison then returned to the lane and nailed his ninth straight strike of the game and thirty-third consecutive strike of the night.

He almost blew his chance at fame on his first ball of the tenth frame. On his release, Allison knew he had pulled his shot and the crowd groaned. Poised at the foul line, the bowler winced as his ball smacked high on the head pin. He thought for sure his strike run was over. But the head pin leaped out of the pack, ricocheted off the side wall, hit the 4-pin, and bumped the last remaining pin, the 9-pin, which wobbled for a breathless second and then fell. The drama left everyone limp with relief and convinced Allison he was destined for perfection.

He calmly rolled the next two balls into the pocket for his thirty-fifth and thirty-sixth consecutive strikes, capping his third straight 300 game and the first 900 series ever in a sanctioned league. Allison had broken the record for the highest series of 886, rolled by Allie Brandt in 1939.

When the final pin fell, Allison did too. Overcome with joy, he crumpled to his knees and had to be helped to his feet by well-wishers. When he finally emerged from the jubilant crowd, tears of happiness were streaming down his face. "There were a lot of grown men who cried that night," one onlooker recalled.

Though Allison's astounding feat was witnessed by more than 250 league bowlers, the ABC refused to honor the record. That's because ABC inspectors checked the surface of Lanes 13 and 14 and concluded that the lane-dressing conditions were not in compliance with ABC regulations.

Bowlers from the leagues and the pro circuit were outraged by the ABC's ruling. Petitions circulated at local lanes, newspaper editorials protested on his behalf, and fellow bowlers chipped in to a "Save the Glenn Allison 900 Fund" to help defray legal costs that the bowler had planned to mount. But it was all to no avail. The ABC still refused to certify the three perfect games. To this day, no one has ever bowled a perfect series sanctioned by the ABC.

Despite the lack of official certification, Allison still basked in the glory of his achievement. A flurry of endorsement offers and interviews came his way, swelling his bank account. And he was showered with praise from all parts of the bowling world.

"Allison's 900 series should go down as one of the greatest feats of all time, like Joe DiMaggio's consecutive game hitting streak," said six-time PBA champion Andy Marzich. "It's like a golfer making ten holes-in-one. It's mind-boggling."

One of the dozens of petitions to the ABC drawn up by league bowlers read: "Glenn Allison's 900 series may never be sanctioned by the ABC, but it will forever be sanctioned in the hearts and minds of millions of bowlers and sports fans as a superb and heroic achievement."

Added Allison, "I know I set the record and no one can take it away from me."

An item printed in an 1897 edition of the New York Bowler's Jour-nal *about a bowler who tried to bowl two times in one week: "Bob Schreyer's better half would not allow him to bowl last Saturday night. She claims that the clause in her marriage contract only stip-ulates he can bowl for one night a week."*

Striking Out

ABC Hall of Famer Chuck Collier holds one of bowling's most bittersweet records—rolling the most number of consecutive strikes without tossing a perfect game.

Believe it or not, Collier fired an astounding twenty-seven straight strikes and didn't end up with a single perfecto.

In 1928, Collier, captain of the Brunswick Mineralite team, agreed to an exhibition match between his squad and a team of local amateur bowlers in Kansas City.

The bowling center was packed with onlookers by the time the local bowlers and Collier arrived. But because of car problems, Collier's teammates were late.

The fans were getting restless over the delay, so Collier suggested that he take on the entire Kansas City team single-handedly by rolling balls for each of his five-member team. His opponents, as well as the crowd, agreed and the match began in earnest.

Collier wowed the crowd by rolling five straight strikes in the first frame. Remarkably, he did the same thing again in the second, third, and fourth frames in all five positions. In the fifth frame, the center erupted in wild cheers when Collier nailed the first four strikes, giving him twenty-four straight—the equivalent of two back-to-back perfect games. He bowed, smiled, and then polished off the frame with another strike.

His perfect run finally ended in the sixth frame. He scored strikes in the first two positions before leaving one standing. The crowd gave Collier a standing ovation for rolling twenty-seven straight strikes. Despite the feat, Collier knew it wouldn't mean much officially because it couldn't be sanctioned by the ABC.

By the time his other teammates arrived, Collier had built a commanding lead, so they let him go ahead and whip the Kansas City opponents by himself.

A Perfect Waste of Time

ABC Hall of Famer Ed Lubanski bowled back-to-back perfect games which were seen by a national television audience—yet, officially, they didn't count.

In 1959, the American Machine and Foundry Company (AMF), makers of automatic pinsetters and bowling balls, sponsored a televised competition with the best bowlers in the company to advertise its products. A three-game series was set up as a scotch doubles match of two four-man teams. In the format, player number one would roll the first ball and continue to bowl as long as he made a strike. If he didn't knock down all ten pins, then player number two would try to pick up the spare and continue bowling until he failed to make a strike. Then the next player on the team would take over, and so on.

All the bowlers seemed confused by the unfamiliar format. With the CBS cameras looking on, Lubanski's team wound up shooting a miserable 149 at the end of the first game.

Embarrassed by their showing in front of a national TV audience, Lubanski was determined to do better. He succeeded beyond his wildest dreams.

As the first bowler up for his team in the second game, Lubanski tossed a strike . . . and another . . . and another. With his teammates cheering him on, he wiped up the lane with a perfect game. He was so hot that he continued his streak in the third game and rolled another 300. He had thrown twenty-four strikes in a row—a feat never before seen on television.

Because of the format, Lubanski's teammates never got the chance to bowl in the final two games. So Lubanski wound up beating the opposing team all by himself to win the series.

As thrilled as he was about the back-to-back perfect games, Lubanski was disappointed when the ABC refused to sanction his achievement because of the event's format.

* * *

Brett Brown, of Middleburg, Virginia, knows exactly how Lubanski felt.

In 1991, Brett and his teammates arrived at the bowling center for a makeup session. But the other team failed to show because of a breakdown in communications. So Brett's team bowled without its opponents present.

In his first game, Brett bowled a 176 and then caught fire. He rolled back-to-back perfect games. But because the 300s were tossed without opposition, the ABC refused to sanction them.

Perfecto!

For most bowlers, rolling a perfect game is an unfulfilled dream. The ABC estimates that an average kegler has a 1 in 34,269 chance of tossing twelve straight strikes in a game. Among the more memorable sanctioned 300s are:

On December, 12, 1990, ABC Hall of Famer Bob Strampe rolled a perfect game—the fifth decade in which he had thrown a 300. "I knew I had one in each of the last four decades," said the sixty-two-year-old bowler, "and I told my wife that I'd like to get one in the 90s before I get too old."

* * *

A teenager rolled the first 300 game in a five-man ABC league. Ernie Fosberg, a former pin-setter from Rockford, Illinois, achieved his perfecto in 1902 using a thirteen-and-a-half-pound wooden ball. For his feat, Ernie received $10 from the ABC. "I used to set pins and take out my pay in bowling," he said at the time. "It looks like it finally paid off."

* * *

Reed Townley, of Gadsen, Alabama, made a dubious record with his 300 game. In 1989, he chalked up the lowest series ever that included a perfect game—476. Incredibly, before tossing his 300, he rolled back-to-back 88s!

* * *

In 1908, the ABC decided to honor the highest-sanctioned league game of the season with a gold medal. Two bowlers from St. Louis, Homer Sanders and A.C. Jellison, had each rolled perfect games that year.

The ABC, however, had only one gold medal. So it ordered Sanders and Jellison to bowl against each other in a three-game series, with the winner getting the medal. Jellison won and was given the gold.

The following year, the ABC decided that any bowler who rolled a sanctioned 300 deserved a gold medal.

* * *

Florida is the home of the oldest and youngest persons to bowl a sanctioned 300. Jerry Wehmann, of Port St. Lucie, was eighty-one years old when he tossed his perfect game in 1992.

"It took me a helluva long time to do it," said Wehmann, a retired real estate broker and a lifelong bowler with a 164 average.

Matt Gilman, of Davie, rolled his perfect game in 1993 at a youth bowling league in Fort Lauderdale. By accomplishing his feat at the age of eleven years and two months, Matt broke the record as the youngest person to toss a 300 game by seven months.

* * *

Valerie Gray of Edinboro, Pennsylvania, has a garage sale to thank for her 300 game in 1992.

"After nine years of using an eight-pound ball, I decided it was time to move on to a ten-pounder," recalled the housewife and mother. "My daughter and I happened to go to a garage sale and I saw this pretty red, white, and blue bowling ball. It was ten pounds and the holes seemed to fit. I bought it for $5." Two months later, she used it to bowl her perfect game.

* * *

The Pollards of Kansas City are the only family with four members who each have tossed 300 games. Daughter Jody got the ball rolling with a perfect game in 1979. Her feat was duplicated by dad Willard in 1981, mom Patricia, also in 1981, and son Patrick in 1982.

* * *

Bob Learn, Jr., of Erie, Pennsylvania, has recorded more sanctioned 300 games than any other ABC member. Learn, who rolled ten perfectos in the 1988–1989 season, had thrown an incredible forty-three perfect games by the end of 1993.

* * *

The latest bowler to roll a sanctioned 300 game left-handed and one right-handed is Kenneth Shaw of Fredricksburg, Virginia. He tossed his perfect game as a lefty in 1983 and as a righty in 1991.

A Heavenly Game

When the Rev. Philip Pavich became the first Catholic priest to roll a 300 in 1963, friends called it a miracle.

Acting as a substitute in a local league, Father Pavich, of Chicago, grabbed an old house ball and then tossed games of 170 and 169. So no one, including the priest himself, thought he would do much better in his final game.

But then he couldn't miss, flinging one strike after another. On his twelfth and final strike, he needed a little divine intervention. "The ball barely touched the head pin on the Brooklyn side," Father Pavich recalled. "But they all went down. Friends told me it must have been a miracle."

Although the priest was offered the ABC's 300 award ring, he had to decline because of church regulations. However, he was allowed to accept a gold belt buckle from the ABC in honor of his feat.

Father Pavich is the only Catholic priest to roll a 300.

A Week Game

Barney Koralewski holds the ABC record for taking the longest time to toss a perfect game—one week!

It happened in 1934 during the second game of a league match when he was a member of the *Buffalo Evening News* bowling team.

"I started with a nice 1–3 pocket hit," Koralewski recalled. "Then on the other alley, I had the same hit. I took it nice and easy and the ball was rolling beautifully. I got eight strikes in a row and had only one Brooklyn Hit."

But then Mother Nature stepped in. Lightning struck a nearby power substation and all the lights in the bowling center went out. The teams waited in the dark for forty-five minutes before league officials announced that they were suspending play for the evening.

Knowing that Koralewski had rolled eight straight strikes, the captain of his team convinced the other squad to wait for an hour in the hopes that the lights would come back on. But by midnight, the power still hadn't been restored, so the captains agreed to finish their session the following week.

"I went home feeling sort of down," Koralewski recalled. "I returned to the alleys the next Thursday night, after having a full week to wonder if I would or wouldn't get four more strikes. I also worried whether or not the ABC would recognize it as a perfect game—that's if I did roll a 300.

"I arrived at the alleys just five minutes before the league starting time. Much to my surprise, there was a crowd which filled the place. The crowd didn't bother me and nobody asked me any questions such as, 'Do you think you can hit the pocket on the first ball?' or 'Are you nervous?'

"None of us was allowed a practice ball because we were resuming our suspended match. Well, I put the ninth ball in there for a strike and had no trouble with the tenth or eleventh.

"Then I got my twelfth straight strike and the crowd let loose. I wasn't excited or nervous. I had worried all those emotions out of me during the week."

Koralewski's only other concern was alleviated when the ABC sanctioned his 300 and sent the bowler his gold medal for a perfect game—the longest in history.

* * *

Koralewski's feat inspired an episode of "The Andy Griffith Show" thirty-three years later, in 1967. On the hit TV show, Mayberry town clerk Howard Sprague, playing in a league, is working on a perfect game when the lights go out. He has to wait a week to resume the game—and gets his 300.

Outta Sight!

Allen Wells threw a perfect game—and never saw a single pin fall.

In 1953, Wells was one of many bowlers who accepted a challenge put forth by the Dunbar Bowling Center in Charleston, West Virginia. The proprietor offered $200 to the person who could bowl the highest three-game series without seeing the pins.

An opaque curtain was placed across the lane halfway between the foul line and the pins. The curtain was just high enough off the floor for the ball to pass underneath. An official was posted near the pits to call out the score after each toss.

Wells, who sported a 190 average in league play, surprised himself when he rolled a 209 in his first effort bowling with a curtain in front of him.

In his second game, he really found the groove. Wells simply couldn't miss, nailing strike after strike. By the time he reached the tenth frame, he was still perfect. The entire bowling center was hushed and many onlookers crowded behind the curtain next to the official scorekeeper to see what Wells couldn't.

With his knees shaking, the bowler drilled two more strikes. Now he needed only one more. Wiping the sweat off his brow and swallowing hard, Wells flung his ball, desperately hoping for his twelfth straight strike.

"It's a strike!" yelled the official from behind the curtain.

The center erupted in cheers as Wells fell to the floor with a mixture of relief and shock. After his friends helped him back to the settee, Wells told them, "There's no way I can top that." He was right. He tossed a 174 in the third game. His 683 series—which included twenty-two strikes and six spares—far outdistanced his nearest competitor's score of 619.

"If I'd known I could bowl that well without seeing the pins, I would've begun bowling blindfolded years ago," said Wells. "You can bet I'm going to bowl without looking from now on."

So Close, Yet So Far

In at least two incredible incidents, bowlers tossed twelve straight strikes in a game and didn't record a 300.

In 1920, Bill Herman, of South Bend, Indiana, hit eleven solid strikes in a row. On his final ball, he leaped for joy when all the pins fell.

But in an incredible stroke of bad luck, one of the pins bounced off the backstop, flew onto the pin deck, and landed standing straight up! According to the rules, it had to be scored as a standing pin.

So even though Herman had knocked over all ten pins, he had to take a score of 299.

* * *

James Blackstone, of Seattle, Washington, knew exactly how Herman felt. In 1905, Blackstone tossed eleven straight strikes. On his last ball, he rolled it right into the pocket. Nine pins went flying. But the ball had sheared the neck off the tenth pin, leaving the base still upright. The rule book stated that it had to be scored as a standing pin. Rather than mark down a 299, Blackstone give himself a score of 299½.

* * *

Charles Gardener and his son George felt the agony of coming oh-so-close to a perfect game.

In 1901 in Indianapolis, Charles was shooting for a 300. On his twelfth toss, he left the 4-pin standing for a 299. Six weeks later, his son George was gunning for a perfect score, having rolled eleven straight strikes. But like father, like son, George knocked down all but one pin on his final throw, leaving the 5-pin. He had to settle for the same score as his father—a 299.

He Just Didn't Have the Heart for It

Most every bowler in the world dreams of tossing a 300 game.

Carl Ulrich had a chance to throw a perfect score—and turned it down.

In 1962, Ulrich, of West Allis, Wisconsin, rolled nine straight strikes. Fellow bowlers on nearby lanes cheered him on as he entered the tenth frame.

Ulrich, who had suffered a heart attack a few years earlier, could feel his heart beating like mad. He stood on the approach, took a few deep breaths, and stared at the tenpins. Then he turned to the other bowlers and said, "Boys, I can't do it. I'm afraid the strain of trying to shoot for a 300 game might be too much for my ticker."

So Ulrich tossed the ball down the lane without aiming and knocked down five pins, to the groans of his companions. He scored a nine in the final frame and finished with a 267.